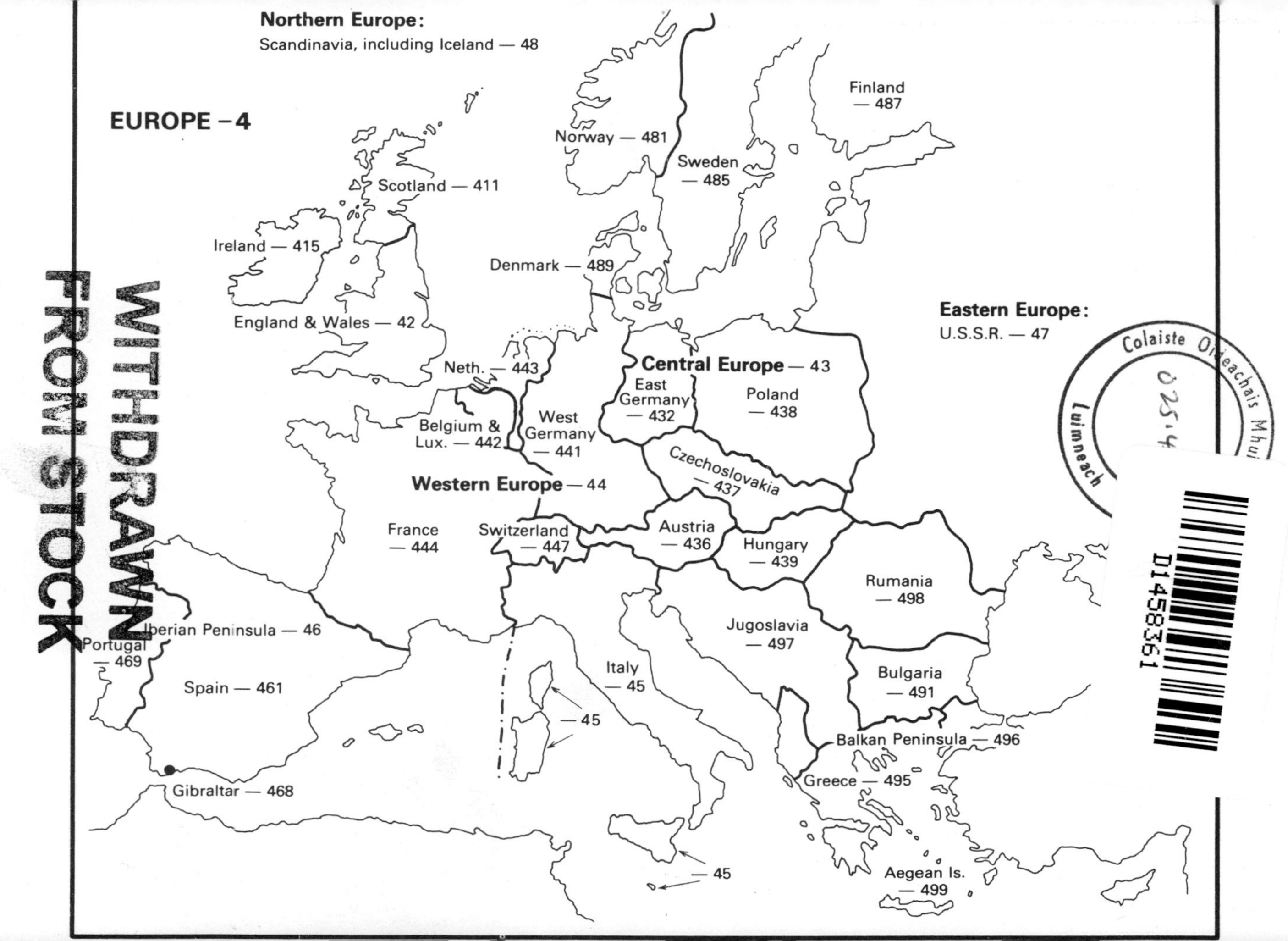
EUROPE – 4
Northern Europe:
Scandinavia, including Iceland — 48
Norway — 481
Sweden — 485
Finland — 487
Scotland — 411
Ireland — 415
Denmark — 489
England & Wales — 42
Eastern Europe:
U.S.S.R. — 47
Central Europe — 43
East Germany — 432
Poland — 438
Neth. — 443
Belgium & Lux. — 442
West Germany — 441
Czechoslovakia — 437
Western Europe — 44
France — 444
Switzerland — 447
Austria — 436
Hungary — 439
Rumania — 498
Iberian Peninsula — 46
Portugal — 469
Jugoslavia — 497
Spain — 461
Italy — 45
— 45
Bulgaria — 491
Balkan Peninsula — 496
Gibraltar — 468
Greece — 495
— 45
Aegean Is. — 499

Introduction to the DEWEY DECIMAL CLASSIFICATION *for British Schools*

Third edition 1977
compiled by

B. A. J. WINSLADE
B.A., A.L.A.

SLA
FOREST PRESS *for the*
SCHOOL LIBRARY ASSOCIATION

First edition (by Marjorie Chambers) 1961
reprinted 1963
Second edition (with minor revisions) 1968
reprinted four times
Third edition (revised and enlarged) 1977

ISBN 0 910608 18 0

Published for the SCHOOL LIBRARY ASSOCIATION
Victoria House, 29–31 George Street, Oxford OX1 2AY
by FOREST PRESS 85 Watervliet Avenue, Albany, New York 12206
Printed and bound in Great Britain at The Pitman Press, Bath

CONTENTS

COMPILER'S FOREWORD

The aim of this *Introduction to the Dewey Decimal Classification* is to help those responsible for administering school library resource centres to use successfully, and with confidence, an internationally accepted scheme of classification.

The explanatory preface covers the basic principles of classification and offers suggestions for adapting the Dewey Decimal Classification to the varying needs of different types of school libraries and for making the most of its flexibility.

In the summaries, tables and schedules special consideration has been given to the needs of schools, where subjects may be studied and interrelated in ways remote from the needs and conceptions of public libraries. As a result there are placements and options that are not offered in the original scheme, which are designed to enable schools to collocate materials on subjects which in their curricula are placed in close relationship – and to do so in accordance with an official adaptation of the Dewey Decimal Classification. It is hoped that this *Introduction* will obviate the need for the more amateur adaptations often found in schools. To obtain maximum benefit from the various options, school librarians will need to be fully conversant with them. They are very strongly urged, therefore, not only to read the preface but also to study closely the tables and schedules before any attempt is made to use the scheme for classification.

Though in this edition the index has been much expanded, its use alone will be insufficient to secure the maximum benefit from the special provisions made for schools.

The first edition of this work, based on the adaptation of the 8th abridged edition of the *Dewey Decimal Classification,* made by Miss Marjorie Chambers for use in the schools of the authority for which she worked, was published with the blessing of Dr Godfrey Dewey in 1961. The present edition, which is based for the most part on the 10th abridged edition, owes much to her original concept, as well as to the many comments of friends and colleagues in the field of school librarianship. The compiler would also like to acknowledge the patient and sympathetic consideration of the particular requirements of schools shown by the publishers of the *Dewey Decimal Classification*. Without such consideration the variations from the order of the original scheme which are to be found in this *Introduction* would not have been possible.

INTRODUCTORY NOTE
by the Chairman of the School Library Association

Previous editions of *Dewey for British Schools* have served their purpose well, as is shown by the steady sales and continuing demand. But neither the world nor the Dewey Classification stands still, and a new edition has become inevitable – indeed overdue. The Association is grateful to Forest Press for renewed permission and support, and to Mr Winslade for undertaking a difficult and laborious task and carrying it out with patience and ingenuity as well as professional skill.

This edition is considerably fuller – and that, we know, will not please everybody. But at least three considerations seem to justify or even demand this expansion. Firstly, the level of expertise among school librarians has steadily risen, and will continue to rise. Secondly, changes in educational methods lend increasing importance to information retrieval and anything that facilitates it. Thirdly, with the enlargement of the library concept to embrace all kinds of non-book material it is desirable to provide a more detailed classification system than books alone might be thought to require.

Therefore we make no apology for this expansion. But we hope that the proper interests of schools seeking something simpler have been safeguarded by the ingenious 'two-tier' scheme adopted. They can confine their attention to the entries underlined (and to the corresponding italics in the index) while being free to draw on the expanded schedules in any sections where their needs, and the size of the stock, make this desirable. We believe that the extremely full index will smooth any apparent difficulties.

It must be stressed that this edition is not simply a revision of the previous one, but a full re-thinking based on the most recent, or forthcoming, full and abridged versions of the Dewey Classification. Many sections are completely recast. One change in particular which may cause some shaking of heads is the 'area' treatment of the British Isles and Europe. This is not a gimmick thought up by the compiler; it is a change now operative in the full scheme, the effects of which are bound to appear increasingly in all libraries and bibliographies. It would have been absurd to turn a blind eye to such changes. Other sections where a new approach has been adopted include music and the very difficult area of social studies.

We welcome and commend the new edition, believing that it will meet the needs of a much wider variety of schools.

Hugh G. Bennett

1 This preface is planned to serve as a guide to the principles and practice of classification for those in charge of school library resource centres. It is of the utmost importance that the advice and instructions given here are thoroughly understood before any attempt is made to use the tables, schedules and index which follow.

2 *The Library*

2:1 Virtually every school, be it primary, middle or secondary, now has a library. Indeed in many places the 'school library' is developing into the 'school library resource centre', concerned with both books and non-book materials. Yet there remain schools in which the need for, and the purpose of, the library that they possess has still to be realised. In others the rapid progress in methods of communication and changes in educational methods are causing new problems of organisation that tend to divert attention from the broader aims of the library and even from the need for one.

2:2 The library resource centre should aim:

(a) To provide as wide a range of materials as possible in support of the work of the school and as recreation material for the pupils;

(b) To awaken and foster interest in those materials, so that pupils become familiar with them as sources of information and pleasure. This will involve not only encouraging children to read by providing an attractive array of books, but also recognising that some children may never be fluent readers and yet may obtain much pleasure and useful information through the use of non-book materials. A tape-recording of a local history item, with appropriate printed materials, may stimulate as much as, if not more than, the printed word alone;

(c) To help children to become more independent in finding and selecting information relevant to a given task or to their own interests and hobbies;

(d) To encourage the exploration of new fields of interest and a deeper sense of involvement in familiar fields.

2:3 To fulfil these aims requires a well planned arrangement of materials in the library resource centre, without which pupils (and staff) will frequently suffer the disappointment of failure to satisfy their needs and/or waste considerable time in trying to do so. Either situation will lead to loss of interest and the needless handling of materials in unguided and haphazard searching. The wise use of a standard classification scheme will help to promote the well planned arrangement that will avoid such prodigality of effort.

3 *Classification*

3:1 Classification involves the grouping together of those items which have certain characteristics in common, and the separation of these from others which do not possess them. For example, one might group a collection of books by colour into, say, red books and blue books. This would be a type of classification. Normally, however, materials are classified in a more generally useful manner. Though a stamp collection might be classified by the colour or shape of the stamps, a more generally useful grouping would be by place of origin. It might also be valuable to further divide the five continental groups (classes) into sub-classes according to country of origin, and perhaps even further by using regional areas (e.g., for Great Britain, using Scotland, Channel Islands etc.). Thus by using the characteristic of territory the collection could be divided into main classes – the continents – each with a number of sub-classes – the individual countries – which in turn were each divided into further sub-classes – the regions. It should be noticed that each sub-class always has the characteristics of all the classes above it: Scotland is not only a part of Great Britain but also a part of Europe. Further subdivision may be made, however, by using characteristics not already employed. For instance a time division (based on date of issue) would create smaller divisions within which the task of finding a specific stamp would be relatively easy. Emphasis has been laid upon the way in which classification enables one to find a particular item in a collection, since this is its prime function.

3:2 In the example given above the physical placing of like object with like object (a stamp of one country with others of the same country) would have been relatively easy because most stamps have the name of their country of origin incorporated in the design.

3:2:1 Otherwise it would have been necessary to invent a code to help in the ordering of the stamps into groups, e.g., *A – Europe*, *B – Asia*, etc. This code could then have been written on the stamps. Such a code is called the *notation*, and would consist of easily recognised signs or symbols used to identify the various classes and sub-classes. A notation should also, however, indicate the relationship of the classes one to another and of the sub-classes to the main class that includes them. For instance, a notation for classifying a stamp collection as outlined above might consist of capital letters to represent the continents (*A – Europe, B – Asia, C – Africa,* etc.) and lower case letters to represent individual countries (*a – Great Britain, b – France, c – Germany,* etc.) with Arabic numerals to represent the regions (*1 – England, 2 – Scotland, 3 – Wales,* etc.) and Roman numerals for the chronological division (e.g., *i – 1830–1900, ii – 1900–1939,* etc.). Thus the notation *Aa2ii* would denote a stamp belonging in the Europe class (*A*), Great Britain sub-class (*a*), Scottish sub-section (*2*), 1900–1939 sub-division (*ii*).

3:2:2 A notation *Ba2ii*, however, might represent a 1930 Manchurian stamp if, in the *B* class (*Asia*) *a* represented China and *2* the Manchurian region. It should be noted that in these two examples, whereas the meanings of *a* and *2* have changed, the meaning of the symbol *ii* has not changed, since it represents a characteristic – the date of issue – that can be common to any stamp no matter where it may originate from; but the *a* and *2* do not represent such a common characteristic, since China is not a part of Europe nor Great Britain a part of Asia. In this instance the Roman numeral notation would represent a *standard subdivision,* which could be applied to any of the other sub-classes in the classification. (Compare Table 1.)

3:2:3 In our example the pages of the stamp album would be marked with the notation devised, and a table or *schedule* would be written out showing all the symbols and the meanings represented by them. Thus the classifier could refer to the schedule for the notation, mark it on the stamp or hinge, and then place the stamp on the appropriate page in the album. Should a stamp fall out of the album it would be easy to replace it correctly by matching the notation on the stamp with that on the page of the album. Thus it can be seen that classification is a means (a) of bringing together those objects that we wish to see together; (b) of indicating, by means of the notation, where they are to be placed relative to one another.

3:3 *Book Classification*

Book classification is based on the principles outlined above and consists of (a) sorting the books into classes *that will be most useful for the people who will wish to use them*; (b) indicating on each book the notation of the class to which the book has been allocated. The notation is usually marked where it is most easily visible, for example on the spine.

3:3:1 It is generally agreed that to group books according to the *subject with which they deal* best meets the needs of the people using them. The Dewey Decimal Classification scheme, devised by Melvil Dewey in 1876 and systematically revised ever since, is an internationally recognised scheme for classification by subject content. The symbols used for the notation are decimal numbers: hence its name.

3:3:2 The scheme divides all knowledge into ten major *classes,* numbered from 0 to 9. Class 0 is used for general works which are not limited to a specific subject, e.g. general encyclopaedias. Each class may have one hundred numbers. Thus class 5 (the pure sciences) covers the numbers 500–599. Each class is separated into ten *divisions*, with general works occupying the first division. Thus the numbers 500–509 stand for the pure sciences in general; 510–519 stand for mathematics; 520–529 for astronomy; 530–539 for physics, and so on. Each division is separated into ten *sections,* of which the first is once again reserved for general works. Thus 510 stands for mathematics in general, 511 for mathematical logic, 512 and 513 for algebra and arithmetic, and so on. Further division into subsections, to any extent that may be desired, can be made by the addition of a decimal point and one or more digits. The main sequence of Melvil Dewey's subdivision of knowledge is shown in the two summaries – one of main *classes,* the other of primary *divisions* – which follow this preface.

3:3:3 Any library item may be classified according to the schedules, each being assigned to the class, division, section or subsection most closely related to its subject matter, *or to the one that will bring it to the eyes of the greatest number of potential users.* It is then marked with the appropriate notation. This *class number* is then used to arrange the materials on the shelves, thus bringing together materials on the same subject and placing them next to those on related subjects. The notation is arranged in numerical order; but since this is a decimal order, subdivisions of a number precede the next whole number – 621.388 precedes 621.4.

3:4 *Non-book Materials*

Non-book materials, which seem to some librarians and teachers to present so many problems, differ little from books, except in their physical format, since – like books – they have a subject content which can be assessed and therefore classified. This being the case it is of great value to the users of the collection if non-book materials are classified according to the same scheme that is applied to the book part of the collection. In this way the user will know where to look for a given subject, even if the non-book materials are stored separately according to format; and the index will be applicable to all the materials in the library resource centre. As with books, these materials may be useful for more than one discipline, so it is imperative that the location (class number) chosen is the one which will bring the material to the attention of as many potential users as possible.

4 *The Dewey Decimal Classification in Schools*

The schedules, tables and index which follow are based mainly on those of the 10th abridged edition of the *Dewey Decimal Classification;* but in some areas – notably social services, pure sciences and music – the compiler has adapted schedules of the full classification, either the 18th edition or the revisions proposed for the 19th (to be published in 1978).* This abridgment has been specially compiled for use in the schools of Great Britain. (With any necessary adjustment to reflect different needs it could be used in the schools of other countries too.)

4:1 This *Introduction* could be used in two ways:

(a) By the teacher-librarian, for whom it will provide the schedules which can be used to classify the materials in the school library resource centre and will also serve as a guide to the compilation of the school's own subject index, which can be based on the index to the schedules. The subject index will often be the first guide to which library users will turn to find the notation assigned to the subject on which they are seeking information. (See 'The use of the index', page 96).

(b) By the class teacher, who can use this shortened version as a guide to the abridged and standard editions. It could also be a valuable aid in training pupils to find all the locations that may be relevant to the given topic.

4:2 *Primary and First School Libraries*

In primary or first schools, the first 'library' that a child will meet is the book corner or class library in the reception and infant classes. Junior and middle schools now frequently aim to acquire a central collection of books – a 'central library' – to supplement or replace the class libraries.

4:2:1 Whilst the number of books in a class library may not appear, at first sight, to warrant detailed classification it will, in the

---

* In the few cases where none of these editions gave rise to a location or notation suitable for schools it was necessary to create numbers which are inevitably at variance with the fuller editions. These are marked by a double asterisk: **

long run, prove more beneficial to view all the books in the school as one collection and to classify them as such. Firstly, the transfer of books between classes will be easier when pupils learn that books on a given subject will always have the same notation, no matter in which classroom they may be housed; secondly, such a classification of the school's collection will facilitate the integration of that collection with materials obtained through the schools service of the public library, so that pupils have available in one sequence the whole range of materials that the school can offer; thirdly, should the collection be centralised at any time, it will be easier to assemble together multiple copies of any item, since they will all bear the same notation instead of being scattered throughout the classification as a result of individual interpretations of the scheme by different teachers.

4:2:2 For pupils in the infant and lower classes of first schools it may be found preferable to use a colour coding scheme. In such a case it will be an advantage if materials are also marked with the notation of the 'First summary (classes)'. These markings may then serve as an introduction to the use of the classification scheme, since the brighter pupils will sooner or later inquire about the significance of the numbers. Where there is extensive use of project and discovery methods of learning, and consequently an enhanced need for pupils to be able to find information for themselves, a fuller classification is needed than can be provided through the use of the first and second summaries, and teachers should turn to the schedules of this *Introduction* as the basis of their classification.

4:2:3 To help teachers in primary and first schools those headings of the tables and schedules thought to be of most use in upper primary and lower middle schools have been underlined in this edition. The corresponding entries in the index are in italics. In addition an optional colour code is provided on page 28.

4:3 *Middle and Secondary (High) Schools*

The schedules and tables that follow should be detailed enough to meet the needs of middle school libraries. Secondary or high school librarians, however, would be well advised to use the abridged edition. In secondary schools which have upper and lower school libraries on separate sites, the lower school library could be classified by this *Introduction*, whilst classification of the upper school library could be based on the abridged edition.

5 *How to Classify*

5:1 The schedules present, in order, the various classes and divisions considered useful in schools, each with the number which constitutes its notation. It is easy to memorise the ten main classes so that, having determined the subject of the item, the classifier can, without recourse to the first summary, place the item in its correct main class. Knowledge of the hundred divisions of the second summary, and of the numerous sections and sub-sections, will be gained gradually as the scheme is used.

5:2 *How to determine the subject of any item*

There are several factors which will help:

(a) *Title* The title usually indicates what the item is about. It is sometimes misleading, however, and some further check should be made.

(b) *Table of contents* This is usually an excellent guide. With non-book materials a table of contents may be found in the accompanying notes. (If there is no table of contents, chapter headings are likely to give a good indication.)

(c) *Preface* It is always wise to read the preface of a book for the author's point of view, even if it merely confirms your decision as to the subject of the book.

(d) *Text* A careful examination of the text will occasionally be necessary for a book but will always be necessary with non-book material.

(e) *Reference books* When the subject is not apparent from an examination of the item, help may often be obtained from other sources, such as catalogues, biographical dictionaries, encyclopaedias, gazetteers and reviews.

(f) *Specialists' opinions* Subject specialists should be consulted when difficulties arise.

5.3 *How to Assign an Appropriate Notation*

Having determined exactly what the item is about, the classifier is ready to classify it, that is to place it in the class, division, section or sub-section *in which it will be most useful to users of that particular library.*

5:3:1 In general an item should always be classified into the most specific group provided in the scheme being used. For example the classifier using this *Introduction* should place materials on football in 796.33, not in the more general class for outdoor ball games 796.3, nor in the still more general class for athletic sports and outdoor games 796. The basic principle is that of usefulness for the clientele of the library concerned. In this respect libraries may differ, and it is the responsibility of the classifier to decide where each item will be of most value for the majority of people using his library. Few materials in a school library present any very complicated problems. It is unlikely that *An outline of world history* would be of more use in any class other than that for world history. But would *Dictators, ancient and modern* be more useful with world history, or politics, or biography? Is a filmstrip on the honey bee more useful with other materials on insects, or with materials on bee-keeping, or with those on foodstuffs? The decision in such cases must be based upon knowledge of the aims of the individual library, which can only by gained by the classifier's own experience, not by any rules set down here.

5:3:2 When any item treats of two subjects, e.g., *A biblical and classical atlas,* it should be assigned to the class in which it will most often be useful. Since all the subjects dealt with (and there will be a number of them in some composite books, e.g., *Arts and industries of modern man*) can be traced through the catalogue by means of extra subject cards, one should always place the item where it will be brought to the attention of the greatest number of potential users. It should be remembered that the notation is primarily a means of providing a shelf location, and that extra catalogue cards, with a 'shelved at' annotation, can be added to guide users to the location chosen. For instance, *Buildings of the Bible* by Ian Calvert could conceivably be classified at either 220 or 726, and will be placed in whichever is thought more convenient for the users of the particular library. An extra catalogue card with class mark written as either $\frac{220}{\text{shelved at 726}}$ or $\frac{726}{\text{shelved at 220}}$ will lead users to the location chosen. If a decision cannot be based on the principle of usefulness, then the materials should be assigned to the class for the first subject treated. When materials treat equally of three or more parts of a larger subject, they should be classified with the larger subject: e.g., a filmstrip dealing with heat, light, sound and mechanics should be placed in the general class 530 Physics.

Translations, reviews, keys, analyses and other works about a particular book should be classed with the original book. For example *Illustrations of the British flora . . . forming a companion to Mr Bentham's handbook,* by W. H. Fitch, should be classified with the book to which it refers, Bentham and Hooker's *Handbook of the British flora*. The history of a subject should be classed with the subject. If there are many books on the subject in the collection it would be advisable to add the standard subdivision—09 to distinguish the historical material from the more general. For example, Edmund Burke's *History of Archery* should be placed with other material on archery in 799.3 (or if preferred 799.309).

5:3:3 Beginners in classification are advised to work step by step with each item as follows:

(a) determine the subject as exactly as possible;
(b) select the appropriate main class from the first summary;
(c) consult the second summary to find the division which contains the subject;
(d) consult the schedules to discover, if possible, a more specific place;
(e) write the notation on the item.

5:3:4 It is of the greatest importance that materials on the same subject, whenever acquired, be kept together and given the same classification number. To ensure this it is necessary to record the decision whenever a classification problem has been settled, so that other materials presenting the same problem at a later date may be treated in the same way. The record should consist of notes inserted in the schedules at the appropriate places. For instance, it may be decided that a filmstrip *What wood is that?* (containing descriptions and photographs of timbers used in furniture making) would be most useful with other materials on woodworking (684). Immediately this decision has been reached a note should be made in the schedules at 684, 'Class here materials on identification of timbers'. A further note should be made in the schedules at 674 (the 'correct' place for materials on timber): 'For identification of timbers see 684'.

5:3:5 To assign materials to a specific class is often difficult. For this reason the schedules have notes in various places either to provide synonyms for the terms used, or to define a term and to indicate its scope – that is, the topics covered by the term used in the schedules. In other places the annotation instructs on the use of specific numbers, or suggested possible alternative numbers (options) which may help to gather in one place materials that would otherwise, by strict adherence to the schedules, be separated. Cross references to related topics are also given.

5:3:6 *Number Building*

The schedules do not list specifically every notation that is possible. To do so would lengthen them unnecessarily, since it is possible to make more specific notations by the use of standard subdivisions added to a base notation. (That is, classes are subdivided according to characteristics that can be applied to them all, e.g., languages by type of material – dictionaries, grammar etc.; literatures by form of material – poetry, drama etc.)

(a) *Use of auxiliary tables.* For example, Table 4 'Subdivisions of individual languages' includes the standard subdivisions —3 dictionaries, —5 grammar, —7 non-standard forms of the language, slang, —8 textbooks. (The dash before the number indicates that the number never stands alone. The dash is omitted in actual use.) Thus German language (base number 43), subdivided by use of the standard subdivisions in Table 4, will give

430 German language
433 German dictionaries
435 German grammar
437 German slang
438 Textbooks for learning German

Where the schedule number does not end in 0 the complete number is used as the base number. Thus

439.3 Dutch language
439.33 Dutch dictionaries
439.35 Dutch grammar
439.38 Textbooks for learning Dutch

(b) *Audio-visual materials (optional notation).* For those librarians who wish to collocate their book and non-book materials but who find that strict collocation (that is, giving a non-book item a class number exactly as if it were a book and shelving it accordingly) would present numerous problems in ensuring that the shelves were kept in order, this *Introduction* provides an optional middle path. By use of the standard subdivisions —022, —023 and —024 (from Table 1) it is possible to locate non-book materials together at the end of the run of books on the same subject. Thus

363.3 Public safety
.3022 Visual materials on public safety
.3023 Audio-visual materials on public safety
.3024 Audio material on public safety
.32 Road safety

.3222*	Visual materials on road safety
.3223*	Audio-visual materials on road safety
.3234*	Audio materials on road safety

However, little is gained by using these notations if catalogue entries clearly indicate (by colour or words) the nature of the material.

Whilst full instructions for use are given at the head of each auxiliary table, all decisions for or against the use of an option should be clearly recorded in the schedules and, if necessary, in the index.

5:4 *Variations from Recommended Practice*

5:4:1 *Officially Recognised Variations*

(a) *Optional placements.* Certain topics are given two (or occasionally more) specific placements in the schedules. One of these is always the editor's 'preferred place' and is the one referred to in the index. In the schedules it will be recognised by the annotation 'If preferred class in . . .' The optional alternative placement carries the annotation 'It is optional to class here . . ., prefer . . .' These alternative placements are offered because there may be legitimate reasons for placing works in non-standard classes in order to locate them near subjects with which they are more closely associated in the school.

(b) *Alternatives for classifying literature.*† The traditional Dewey division of literature, as shown in Table 3, is into groups based on the form of writing used, e.g., drama, poetry etc. This has the disadvantage of splitting up the works of an author who writes in more than one form. For example Shakespeare's plays would be classed at 822 whereas his poetry would be at 821. A solution to this problem is provided through the use of the option 'If preferred all works, regardless of form, may be classed in —8 (the miscellaneous works subdivision) or in the

---

* Strictly these numbers should be 363.32022 to 362.32024, but in order to shorten them the initial 0 of the standard subdivisions has been omitted. This is only possible where it does not cause confusion. For instance to try to shorten the numbers for non-book materials on public safety in this way would result in the notations 362.322 to 362.324: this could obviously cause confusion since these numbers appear to refer to road safety. Similarly a library possessing items on museums of mammals could create a sub-class with the notation 599.074 (599 Mammals, and standard subdivision —074 Museums); but to try to shorten this by omitting the 0 would lead to confusion, since 599.74 is used in the schedules for carnivorous animals. All notations created by number building should be checked against the schedules to ensure that the notation created has not already been used for another sub-class.

† Popular modern literature — fiction — is most frequently shelved in a separate sequence organised alphabetically by author's surname.

base number for the literature (adding 0 when required to make a three-digit number)'. All Shakespeare's works would then be classed at 828 or 820.

Under each of these options the sequence would be alphabetical according to the first three letters of the author's surname. For example use of option 1 would result in

821 OWE The poetry of Wilfred Owen
821 POP The poetry of Alexander Pope
821 POW The poetry of W. Cowper Powys
821 ROS The poetry of D. G. Rossetti
821 SEW The poetry of Anna Seward
821 SHA The poetry of William Shakespeare
822 MAR The plays of Christopher Marlowe
822 OCA The plays of Sean O'Casey
822 PIN The plays of Harold Pinter
822 PRI The plays of J. B. Priestley

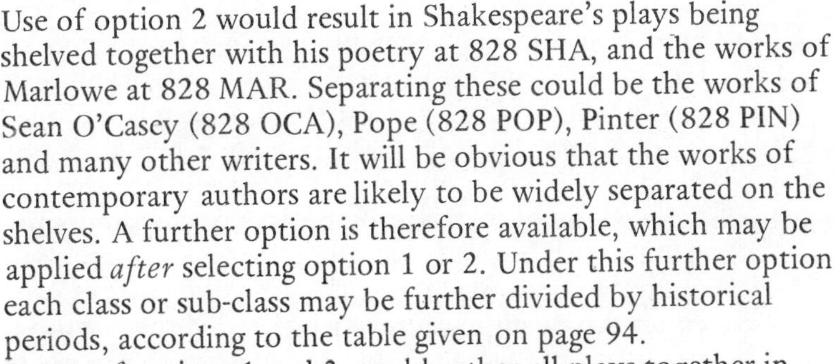

Use of option 2 would result in Shakespeare's plays being shelved together with his poetry at 828 SHA, and the works of Marlowe at 828 MAR. Separating these could be the works of Sean O'Casey (828 OCA), Pope (828 POP), Pinter (828 PIN) and many other writers. It will be obvious that the works of contemporary authors are likely to be widely separated on the shelves. A further option is therefore available, which may be applied *after* selecting option 1 or 2. Under this further option each class or sub-class may be further divided by historical periods, according to the table given on page 94.

Use of options 1 and 3 would gather all plays together in sub-class 822, with subdivision by periods: thus the plays of Shakespeare and Marlowe would be close together at 822.3 and separated from those of, say, J. B. Priestley at 822.912. Similarly Shakespearean poetry at 821.3 would be separated from that of Wilfred Owen, W. Cowper Powys and their contemporaries, which would be together at 821.9.

Use of options 2 and 3 would place Elizabethan literature at 828.3 (or 820.3) and separate it from that of the immediate post-Victorians (Owen, Powys, Priestley) at 828.9 (or 820.9), and further separate these from the moderns (O'Casey, Pinter etc.) gathered together at 828.94 (or 820.94).

It is therefore possible to choose either to separate a literature collection into a number of sub-classes according to the forms in which it is written, or to keep the collection together as a single sub-class. Having made this decision, one can then choose to keep each sub-class thus formed as one, organised alphabetically, or to subdivide the sub-classes chronologically in order to bring together the works of contemporary authors.

(c) *Alternatives for classifying geography.* Traditionally in the Dewey Decimal Classification the various branches of geography have been placed under specific topics that have then been considered by area using the standard subdivision –09 from Table 1: e.g., 330 Economics, 330.9 Economic geography; 580 Botany, 580.9 Plant geography. However, many teachers of geography naturally prefer materials related to their subject to be shelved together. Such an arrangement of 'topical' geography is given an optional placement at 910.1, under the instruction 'Add 001–899 to the base number 910.1.' Thus: economic geography = geography (910.1) + economics (330), i.e., 910.133; plant geography = geography (910.1) + botany (580), i.e., 910.158; physical geography = geography (910.1) + earth science (550), i.e., 910.155. The geography of non-political areas (e.g., deserts, tropics, hemispheres, oceans) is placed at 910.9; historical geography at 911; atlases and maps at 912; and general geography, arranged according to political regions, occupies 914 to 919. Thus by using this option the whole range of geographical materials can be grouped together.

(d) *Area subdivision.* Occasionally it may be useful to subdivide a collection of material on a topic by areas. For instance, a collection of materials on birds may contain items dealing mainly with birds of a certain country or area, to which it is desired to draw attention. The schedule number can be regarded as a base number to which is added the notation for area treatment (–09 from Table 1) followed by the notation for the specific area from Table 2:

598.2	Birds: general treatment
598.29*	Geographical treatment of birds
598.294*	Birds of Europe
598.2941*	Birds of Great Britain

As a help in classifying by area, maps marked with the area notation are printed on the endpapers of this book.

(e) *Alternatives for classifying biography.* In some libraries biographical materials may be best arranged by bringing them all together at one location; whereas in others an arrangement which links materials about a person with those on the subject with which he is most associated may be more suitable. Both such arrangements are possible.

* See footnote, p. 16.

Where all biographical materials are gathered together some arrangement for obtaining a shelf order is needed. An alphabetical arrangement based on the surname of the biographee has the advantage of bringing together all biographical (and autobiographical) works about an individual. In the Dewey Classification this type of arrangement is supplied by the division 920, under which may be placed all biographical materials dealing with individuals, the shelf order being obtained by adding, after 920, the first three letters of the biographee's surname. (See paragraph 5:5.) Thus materials about Henry Ford would be given the notation 920 FOR. Collected biography (i.e., materials dealing with the lives of a variety of persons) could be placed at 920 without added notation.

If it is desired to relate biographical materials to the subject of the main life's work of the biographee, the option given at 920 – to classify such materials with the subject, adding the standard subdivision –092 – should be taken up. A book on Einstein would be classed at 510.92; one on Henry Ford, or *Pioneers of the motor-car*, at 629.2092. Such an arrangement, however, separates general collected biography, which would be at 920, from the main bulk of biography which would be spread through the subject divisions.

A further option, which would keep all biography together, placing collected biography at 920 followed immediately by individual biography divided according to the subject of the biographee's work, is also possible. Treating the division for biography as a base number (i.e., 92) and dividing by subject, one would obtain a schedule for biography of which part is given below as an example:

920	Collected biography
920.7	Biographies of famous journalists
921	Biographies of philosophers
922.2	Biographies of biblical characters
922.35	Biographies of saints
922.66	Biographies of missionaries
923.013	Biographies of archaeologists
923.21	Biographies of monarchs and statesmen
923.61	Biographies of social workers
923.88	Biographies of famous road builders

and so on up to 928.9 (the notation 929 has a different significance). It is vital that whichever method is adopted should be applied to all biographical materials consistently, and that the schedules should be marked to show which system is being followed.

5:4:2 *Unofficial Variations*

It has been suggested that, for some school libraries, even this *Introduction* may prove to be too detailed. For instance, when classifying the several hundred items in the central library of a primary school, one may decide to use only the headings of the second summary, rather than those headings of the schedules recommended by underlining (see paragraph 4:2:3). Before such partial use of the scheme is decided upon, however, the full schedules should be very carefully examined. If, as is likely, it seems that the library may in time acquire a number of items on a subject (e.g., animals), it would be prudent to adopt a closer classification and division of the subject. Indiscriminate broad classifying may create difficulties for a child who requires material on a more specific subject. He will find it very frustrating to have to search through 60–70 books loosely classified under 'animals' when he really requires material on monkeys. It may also mean that at some future date the librarian, or his successor, will be faced not only with the task of adding decimal points and a figure, but also with the more difficult task of replacing the final 0 by another figure, and doing this not only on the materials themselves but on every record relating to them.

If, despite the warning given in the last paragraph, the librarian of a junior school decides to use the second summary, but foresees that (for example) the main class 900 (History geography, biography) is likely to expand more than any other, he will find it necessary to use part of the full schedules along with the second summary. Only by doing so will he be able to obtain the division of modern history and geography by country that he will almost certainly require. To ensure consistent procedure, by himself and his successors, he should mark the classification scheme both in the second summary and at the appropriate sections of the schedules. The second summary should be marked, for example, as below:

940 Europe SEE 940–949 in schedules
940 Asia SEE 950–959 in schedules
960 Africa SEE 960–969 in schedules

As a general rule the middle and secondary school librarian will need to use the full schedules. Should, however, a decision be made to cut back the schedules, for instance to eliminate the period divisions in history, the parts of the schedule thus made redundant must be marked boldly, in the manner shown below, to ensure consistency in the use of the notation.

	941	HISTORY OF BRITISH ISLES
941	.**Ø1**	Early history
941	.**Ø6**	Act of Union
941	.**Ø7**	Georgian period House of Hanover
941	.**Ø8**	Victorian era to present day
941	.**Ø81**	Victoria, 1837–1901

and so on.

5:4:3 The librarian must always take into account any special courses being offered in the school, which will naturally be reflected in the stock of the school library. For example, a school with a pre-nursing course might acquire a considerable stock in the medical section of the library. In such a case the librarian would be well advised to study the classes 610–619 in both the 10th abridged and the 18th standard edition with a view to the possible expansion of the schedules for these particular classes. Should some expansion be needed the appropriate part of the adopted schedules would have to be copied and interleaved at the appropriate place. At the same time classes 610–619 in the schedules of the *Introduction* would have to be scored through, and a note appended, 'See expanded schedule attached.'

When any such expansion is made particular attention should be paid to any cross-references in the adopted schedule. Each reference should be checked to verify that it leads to a notation used in this *Introduction.* If it does not, then either the notation referred to or the reference itself should be amended. For instance, in the 10th abridged edition at 612.6 (Reproduction, development, maturation) there is a cross-reference, 'Class a specific aspect of sex with the subject, e.g., sex psychology, 155.3.' This notation does not exist in the schedules of this *Introduction.* The reference would have to be amended to read 'e.g., sex psychology, 150', or the schedules of this *Introduction* would have to be expanded at 150 Psychology to include the notation 155.3 Sex psychology.

Similarly any cross-references in the rejected portions must be checked to verify that any reference to them from elsewhere in the schedules would lead to the appropriate point in the adopted schedule. For instance, in this *Introduction* at 613.2 (Dietetics) there is a note, 'If preferred class slimming in 646.7.' This option does not exist in the 10th abridged edition (having been written in especially for schools to facilitate the assembling of relevant materials for those with a personal hygiene course). If the abridged edition schedules were adoped, either the reference would have to be written into the adopted schedules, or the reference, 'It is optional to class here slimming, prefer 613.2', which occurs at 646.7 in the schedules of this *Introduction,* would have to be deleted.

Also requiring attention when the schedules are expanded or condensed is the subject index. Every subject name affected, its synonyms and cross-references need to be examined, and the notation checked and if necessary altered. It is essential that every reference should be checked to ensure that it corresponds with the remainder of the schedules.

5:5 *Notation for Changes*

This *Introduction,* with the various options described above, should suffice to cater for almost every need – or whim. But any librarian who feels that a particular need would be better served by some arrangement other than that provided should use a distinctive notation. This can be done by using the letters of the alphabet, inserted before or after the Dewey notation or substituted for it: for instance, R for reference books not to be removed from the library, M for music scores, B for individual biography and F for fiction in, or translated into, English.

5:6 A most important point, to be borne in mind at all times, is that the classifier is establishing an arrangement that will be used by his successors and by generations of pupils. Unless every deviation is clearly recorded at every point affected, these people will suffer almost as much frustration and waste of time as if the library had not been classified at all.

6 *Dewey for the Class and Specialist Teacher*

Whilst there will normally be only one member of the school staff concerned with the actual classification of library materials, every member of the staff will want to use those materials, and needs therefore to be familiar with their arrangement. Equally, though the librarian will take every opportunity of training all pupils in the use of the library, whenever any child happens to be at a loss or uncertain where to find what he wants, he may rightly expect any member of the staff to help him. It would therefore be useful if a copy of the classification scheme could be easily accessible to every teacher. In secondary schools copies could with advantage be provided in subject rooms to help specialist teachers to exploit the library to the full.

6:2 The Dewey schedules form a chart of knowledge. The

specialist teacher will wish to know where his own subject fits into the scheme, and its relationship with other subjects. To secure full benefit from the library he needs to have a general knowledge of the structure of the whole scheme and a special knowledge of the parts which deal with his own subject and related aspects of other subjects. Each teacher needs to be fully and constantly aware of the possibilities of the library resource centre; he needs to remind his pupils (and occasionally himself) of the many approaches to a subject, of the many links between one subject and another.

6:3 The whole body of knowledge has to be broken down to make it manageable for teaching and learning. In the library the separated elements are fused together again. Every librarian knows that this reunification does not happen automatically. A child at school, or an adult using a public or academic library, may visit the same section of the library for years without having a clear conception of what materials the rest of the shelves hold. The librarian will try to draw attention to the diversity of the stock by good signposting and display, but success will only be achieved when everyone guiding people to materials in the library can do so not in one section only but in all. In a school this means that every member of the staff should be able to give some guidance in the use of the library.

6:4 The specialist teacher will find the subject index a useful and speedy pointer to the borderline topics which his own subject may share with others. For example, without reference to the index the craft teacher might miss items on the production of pottery dealt with from an industrial angle. The index brings together the various aspects of the subject and shows where they are to be found in different parts of the classification. For this reason, in both the full and abridged editions, it is always referred to as a 'relative index'. It is probably this relative index that will be the part of this *Introduction* most used by the teaching staff. It should certainly be used by every teacher who expects his pupils to read widely around the subject he is teaching them. A copy (or several copies) should be easily available.

A full explanation of the subject index and how to use it precedes the index itself.

FIRST SUMMARY: CLASSES

000 GENERAL WORKS

100 PHILOSOPHY

200 RELIGION

300 SOCIAL SCIENCES

400 LANGUAGE

500 PURE SCIENCES

600 TECHNOLOGY (APPLIED SCIENCES)

700 THE ARTS AND RECREATION

800 LITERATURE

900 HISTORY, GEOGRAPHY, BIOGRAPHY

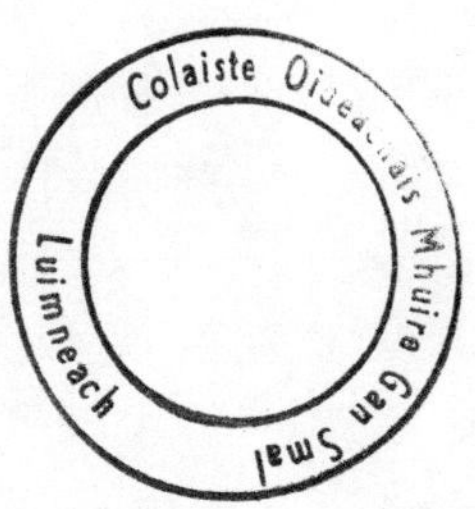

SECOND SUMMARY: DIVISIONS

000 GENERAL WORKS

020 LIBRARY SCIENCE
030 GENERAL ENCYCLOPAEDIAS

050 GENERAL SERIAL PUBLICATIONS
060 MUSEUM SCIENCE
070 JOURNALISM

090 MANUSCRIPTS

100 PHILOSOPHY

110 METAPHYSICS
120 KNOWLEDGE, CAUSE, PURPOSE, MAN
130 POPULAR PSYCHOLOGY

150 PSYCHOLOGY
160 LOGIC
170 ETHICS
180 ANCIENT & MEDIEVAL PHILOSOPHY
190 MODERN & WESTERN PHILOSOPHY

200 RELIGION

210 NATURAL THEOLOGY
220 BIBLE
230 CHRISTIAN DOCTRINE
240 CHRISTIAN DEVOTION AND PRAYER
250 RELIGIOUS ORDERS
260 WORK OF THE CHRISTIAN CHURCH
270 CHRISTIAN CHURCH HISTORY
280 CHRISTIAN CHURCHES & SECTS
290 OTHER RELIGIONS

300 SOCIAL SCIENCES

310 SOCIAL STATISTICS
320 POLITICAL SCIENCE
330 ECONOMICS
340 LAW
350 PUBLIC ADMINISTRATION
360 SOCIAL WELFARE
370 EDUCATION
380 COMMUNICATIONS, TRANSPORT
390 CUSTOMS & FOLKLORE

400 LANGUAGE

410 LINGUISTICS
420 ENGLISH LANGUAGE
430 GERMANIC LANGUAGES
440 FRENCH LANGUAGE
450 ITALIAN LANGUAGE
460 SPANISH & PORTUGUESE LANGUAGES
470 LATIN
480 GREEK (CLASSICAL AND MODERN)
490 OTHER LANGUAGES

500 PURE SCIENCES

510 MATHEMATICS
520 ASTRONOMY
530 PHYSICS
540 CHEMISTRY
550 EARTH SCIENCES
560 PALAEONTOLOGY
570 ANTHROPOLOGY & BIOLOGY
580 BOTANY
590 ZOOLOGY

600 TECHNOLOGY (APPLIED SCIENCES)

610 MEDICAL SCIENCE
620 ENGINEERING
630 AGRICULTURE, FOOD PRODUCTION
640 HOME ECONOMICS, HOUSECRAFT
650 BUSINESS AND BUSINESS METHODS
660 CHEMICAL TECHNOLOGY
670 PROCESSING TRADES
680 CRAFT TRADES
690 BUILDING

700 THE ARTS

710 CIVIC AND LANDSCAPE ARTS, PLANNING
720 ARCHITECTURE
730 SCULPTURE
740 DRAWING, DECORATIVE ARTS, DESIGN
750 PAINTING
760 PRINTS & PRINT MAKING
770 PHOTOGRAPHY
780 MUSIC
790 RECREATIONS, HOBBIES, SPORTS

800 LITERATURE

810 AMERICAN LITERATURE
820 ENGLISH LITERATURE
830 GERMANIC LITERATURE
840 FRENCH LITERATURE
850 ITALIAN LITERATURE
860 SPANISH & PORTUGUESE LITERATURE
870 LATIN LITERATURE
880 GREEK LITERATURE
890 OTHER LITERATURES

900 HISTORY, GEOGRAPHY, BIOGRAPHY

910 GEOGRAPHY, TRAVELS, DESCRIPTION
920 BIOGRAPHY
930 ANCIENT HISTORY
940 HISTORY OF EUROPE
950 HISTORY OF ASIA
960 HISTORY OF AFRICA
970 HISTORY OF NORTH AMERICA
980 HISTORY OF SOUTH AMERICA
990 HISTORY OF OTHER REGIONS

000	Reference	Grey
100 200	Philosophy Scripture	Black
300	Public services Transport Folk tales	Orange
400	Language	Brown
500 550 551	Sciences Earth sciences Weather	Yellow
560	Prehistoric animals	Yellow
570	Nature study in general	Green
580	Plants, trees, flowers	Green/red
590	Animals and birds	Green/gold
600 630 640 650-690	Technology Agriculture, farming The home Industries	Red
700 720 750 780 790	The arts Architecture, castles houses Painting Music Recreation, games, sports hobbies	Mauve
800	Plays, poetry	Brown
900 910 920 930-990	General history General geography Biography History and geography of specific countries	Blue

SCHEDULES

USE OF THE SCHEDULES

General instructions for the use of the schedules are given in the preface, section 5.

The co-ordinate or subordinate relationship between subjects is shown partly by the degree of indentation and partly by the relative length of the notation.

Entries and headings underlined in the schedules are those thought likely to provide for the needs of primary and middle schools. The corresponding entries in the index are in italics, with the class number on the left.

Italics in the schedules refer the user from one part of the schedules to another, either pointing to an alternative placement for the topic or leading to a related topic.

A double asterisk following a number indicates that the notation differs from the full and abridged editions: see footnote, page 10.

GENERAL WORKS

000 GENERAL WORKS

001 GENERAL KNOWLEDGE

.5 Information and communication

Including codes and ciphers

.53 Cybernetics

Communication through verbal and non-verbal language; methods of storing knowledge through written and other records; Audio and visual media as methods of communication

For the media as public entertainment, see 791.4

.6 Data processing

Nonmechanised, automatic, electronic

Including the use of computers

If preferred class use of computers in 519.4

020 LIBRARY SCIENCE

Including educational use, administration, description of libraries of all kinds

Class here guides on how to use the library

028 READING AND READING GUIDANCE

Including discussion of children's books, lists of books, collections of book reviews not limited to any one subject and designed as aids in the selection of individual reading

Class studies of children's literature in 828

.7 Use of books and other forms of recorded knowledge as sources of information

Including guides to study and research

030 GENERAL ENCYCLOPAEDIAS AND YEAR BOOKS

Class encyclopaedias and year books devoted to a specific subject in the general class for the subject plus 'standard subdivision' -03, eg., encyclopaedia of mythology, 290.03

050 GENERAL SERIAL PUBLICATIONS

Class here school magazines

060 MUSEUM ORGANISATION

Class here general works on museums

Class museums related to a specific subject in the general class for the subject, plus 'standard subdivision' -074, eg., ornithological museums, 598.2074

070 JOURNALISM

Including managing, editing, producing, writing for periodicals and newspapers; law of the press; newspapers themselves, radio and television newsreels; documentaries

.5 Book publishing

090 MANUSCRIPTS

Class here school records (day-books etc)

PHILOSOPHY

100 PHILOSOPHY

109 HISTORY OF PHILOSOPHY

110 METAPHYSICS

111 ONTOLOGY
Nature and relations of being

.1 Existence and the essence of being
.8 Transcendental properties of being
Unity, truth, goodness, evil, beauty (aesthetics)

113 COSMOLOGY
Origin of the universe and life

115 TIME, DURATION, ETERNITY
Including the relation of time and motion, space-time, implications of theories of relativity
For measurement of time, see 529

120 KNOWLEDGE, CAUSE, PURPOSE, MAN

126 CONSCIOUSNESS AND PERSONALITY (THE SELF)

127 THE UNCONSCIOUS AND THE SUBCONSCIOUS

128 MAN
His soul, mind, nature, death
For Christian view of death, see 236

129 ORIGIN AND DESTINY OF INDIVIDUAL SOULS
Incarnation, re-incarnation, immortality
For Christian view of immortality, see 236

130 POPULAR PSYCHOLOGY, OCCULTISM

133 PARA-PSYCHOLOGY AND OCCULTISM
For superstition, folklore, see 398; apparitions, ghosts, 398.2; mirages, 551.5

.3 Divinatory arts
Including fortune telling, crystal gazing
.4 Magic, witchcraft, demonology
Including voodooism, good-luck
.5 Astrology
Including zodiac signs, horoscopes, birthstones
For astronomy, see 520
.8 Extra-sensory perception
Including telepathy, clairvoyance
.9 Spiritualism

150 PSYCHOLOGY

153 INTELLIGENCE, INTELLECTUAL AND CONSCIOUS MENTAL PROCESSES
.1 Memory and learning
.8 Will
Including choice and decision, persuasion, brain-washing

154 SUBCONSCIOUS STATES AND PROCESSES

.3 Daydreams, fantasies, reveries, hallucinations
.6 Sleep, dreams, somnambulism
.7 Hypnotism

155 INDIVIDUAL PSYCHOLOGY, INDIVIDUAL BEHAVIOUR
For social psychology, see 302

160 LOGIC

Science of reasoning

170 ETHICS

Conduct and morals

180 ANCIENT AND MEDIEVAL PHILOSOPHY

181 ORIENTAL PHILOSOPHY

Including philosophy based on specific religion, eg., Judaism

183 ANCIENT GREEK PHILOSOPHY

187 ANCIENT ROMAN PHILOSOPHY

190 MODERN WESTERN PHILOSOPHY

RELIGION

200 RELIGION

210 NATURAL THEOLOGY

Religious theories, eg., deism, agnosticism, atheism, humanism, pantheism

215 SCIENCE AND RELIGION

Class here interdisciplinary works on evolution

220 THE BIBLE

Including collected bible stories

For Old Testament only, see 221; New Testament, 225

.2 Concordances and indexes of the Bible

.3 Dictionaries and encyclopaedias of the Bible

.5 Texts of the Bible

Including modern versions

.7 Commentaries

Criticism and interpretation arranged in textual order with or without accompanying text

.9 Biblical geography and history

.92 Biblical biography

Including bible stories about specific people

221 OLD TESTAMENT

Including collected Old Testament stories

Divide like 220, eg., Text of the Old Testament, 221.5; story of Noah and the Ark, 221.92

222 SPECIFIC PARTS OF THE OLD TESTAMENT

eg., Psalms

225 NEW TESTAMENT

Including collected New Testament stories

Divide like 220, eg., Text of the New Testament, 225.5; story of St Peter, 225.92

If preferred class lives of biblical saints with spiritual beings in 235

For stories of Christ and the Holy Family, see 232

226 SPECIFIC PARTS OF THE NEW TESTAMENT

eg., Gospels, Acts, Epistles

230 CHRISTIAN DOCTRINE

231 GOD, THE HOLY TRINITY

232 JESUS CHRIST, HIS LIFE AND TEACHING

.9 Christ's life and his family

For general works on Christmas, Easter, see 263.9

235 SPIRITUAL BEINGS

Saints, angels, devils

It is optional to class here lives of biblical saints prefer 225

236 DEATH, LIFE AFTER DEATH

See also, 128 and 129

240 CHRISTIAN DEVOTION AND PRAYER

The practice of the Christian religion

242 DEVOTIONAL LITERATURE

Prayers for individuals and families, private worship

245 *It is optional to class here Hymns and Carols: prefer 782.27/782.28*

247 CHURCH FURNISHINGS

250 RELIGIOUS ORDERS

Bishops, pastors, priests

see also, 262; 280

255 CLOSED RELIGIOUS ORDERS

Monks, nuns

Class here monasteries, nunneries, convents

260 WORK OF THE CHRISTIAN CHURCH

Institutions, services, observances, disciplines, work of the church

262 CHURCH GOVERNMENT

Episcopacy, synods

For the Papacy, see 282.09

263 DAYS, TIMES, PLACES OF RELIGIOUS OBSERVANCE

.042 Shrines, holy places

Class here pilgrims and pilgrimages

.9 The church's year

264 PUBLIC WORSHIP; CHRISTIAN RITUAL AND LITURGY

266 MISSIONS AND MISSIONARY SOCIETIES

267 ASSOCIATIONS FOR RELIGIOUS WORK

Salvation Army, YMCA

270 CHRISTIAN CHURCH HISTORY

274-279 Church history by continent, country, locality

Add 'Areas' notation -4-9 from Table 2 to base number 27, eg., Church in Europe, 274

280 CHRISTIAN CHURCHES AND SECTS

281 PRIMITIVE AND ORIENTAL CHURCHES

For early Christian church, see 270

.9 Eastern Orthodox churches

282 ROMAN CATHOLIC CHURCH

.09 The Papacy

283 THE ANGLICAN COMMUNION

284 EUROPEAN PROTESTANT CHURCHES

Baptist, Lutheran, Methodist, Pentecostal, Unitarian, United Reform

289 OTHER DENOMINATIONS AND SECTS

.3 Latter day saints (Mormons)

.5 Christian Scientists

.6 Society of Friends (Quakers)

.9 Others

Including Jehovah's Witnesses

290 OTHER RELIGIONS AND MYTHOLOGY

Class here collected mythology

If preferred class mythology in 398 or 930

For folklore, folktales, legends, see 398

291 COMPARATIVE RELIGION

292 GREEK AND ROMAN MYTHOLOGY AND RELIGION

If preferred class in 937 and 938 or collectively in 398

.937 Roman mythology

see also Roman literature 880

.938 Greek mythology

see also Greek literature 870

293 GERMANIC MYTHOLOGY

If preferred class in 936.3 or in 398

.5 Norse mythology

If preferred class in 936 or 398

294 RELIGIONS OF INDIC ORIGIN

.3 Buddism

.5 Hinduism

296 JUDAISM

297 ISLAM

298 Use for religions not specified in this table

299 FAR EASTERN RELIGIONS

Taoism, Confucianism

SOCIAL SCIENCES

300 SOCIAL SCIENCES

Sciences dealing with social activities and institutions

301 SOCIOLOGY

.01 Philosophy and theory

.7 Kinds of societies

Class here general works on primitive, advanced societies, eg., sociological works on the Incas

302 SOCIAL INTERACTION

Including social psychology (Study of collective responses and behaviour of groups)

For individual psychology, see 155

.2 Social communication

.23 Mass communication

The mass media and their audiences

For the mass media as entertainment, see 791.4

.3 Interpersonal relationships

Person to person, person to group, group to group personal relations and attitudes

Class here general works on personal development

If preferred class race relations in 303.6

.5 Relationship of individual to society

For relationship of individual to the state, see 323

303 SOCIAL PROCESSES

.3 Social control

Including propaganda, socialisation

.38 Public opinion

.4 Social change

Including changes induced by contact with other cultures

.6 Social conflict

Riots, revolutions, uprisings

It is optional to class here comprehensive works on race relations: prefer 302.3; specific works on racial discrimination, apartheid: prefer 305

.64 Civil war

.66 War

Sociological treatment

For military aspects, see 355.02

304 FACTORS RELATED TO SOCIAL PROCESSES

.2 Ecology

Influence and effect of environment on human groups

Class here interdisciplinary works on conservation and pollution

For soil conservation, see 631.4; conservation of specific areas, 333.7; works on the 'Third World', underdeveloped countries, 327

Specific aspects of pollution are classed with the subject, eg., pollution of rivers, 910.916

.4 Population

.42 Growth and decline; density

.46 Population control

Including sociological aspects of birth control

For physical aspects, see 613.9; moral aspects, 170; religious viewpoint, 215

304.49 Population distribution

Add 'Areas' notation -1-9 from Table 2 to base number 304.49, eg., population distribution in Great Britain, 304.4941; population distribution in Africa, 304.496

For ethnography, see 572.9

.8 Movement of populations

Including emigration, immigration, internal migration

305 SOCIAL STRUCTURE

Social status; social problems (including prejudice, discrimination, segregation, apartheid)

If preferred class racial segregation, apartheid in 303.6

.2 Specific age levels

Children, adolescents, adults, aged; child rearing

If preferred class child rearing in 649

.5 Social classes

.56 Lower (labouring) classes; alienated and excluded classes, eg., gypsies, tramps, hippies

For general works on the poor, see 339; general works on the 'Third World', 327; social services to the poor, 362.2

306 CULTURE AND CULTURAL PROCESSES

Beliefs, mores, customs

Class here cultural and social anthropology, comprehensive works on anthropology

For physical anthropology, see 572

.1 Minority groups

.7 The sexes and their relations

If preferred class sex education in 613.9 or 646.7

.8 Marriage and family life

Including divorce, intrafamily relationships, the 'generation gap'

307 COMMUNITIES, COMMUNITY LIFE

.3 Living conditions

Class here general works on housing, accommodation, slum clearance

.7 Specific kinds of communities

Including communes, kibbutzes

.72 Rural communities, village life

.76 Urban communities, town life

308** SOCIAL AND FORMAL CONDUCT

Including social etiquette

For etiquette of dining and entertaining, see 642

310 SOCIAL STATISTICS

For demography see 304.4; ethnography 572.9

320 POLITICAL SCIENCE

.5 Political theories

Including communism, fascism

321 FORMS OF STATES

Federal states, empires, monarchy; oligarchy, democracy, ideal states - utopias; anarchy; feudal system; despots, tyrants; communist and fascist states

For theory of communism, fascism, see 320.5

323 INTERNAL RELATIONS OF STATES
Relation of state to the individual

.4 Civil and human rights

326 SLAVERY AND EMANCIPATION

327 INTERNATIONAL RELATIONS

.2 The world community
Political affairs of the world community; 'Third World'; developing countries; international political organisations
For international economic organisations, see 330.6206

.22 League of Nations
.23 United Nations
Including subsidiary bodies
.24 Regional political associations and organisations, eg., The Arab League
.25 Extra-regional political organisations and associations eg., NATO

.7 International co-operation
Including international judicial co-operation; international economic law
Class here international and overseas aid
For international economic organisations, see 330.6206

328 LEGISLATION
For government, see 351-352; civil and international law, 340
It is optional to class here central government and parliamentary law: prefer 351

329 PRACTICAL POLITICS
Including political parties and electoral processes
.9 Geographical treatment
Use 329 for political parties, electoral processes of own country.
For political parties, electoral processes of other countries add 'Areas' notation -4-9 from Table 2 to base number 329.9, eg., practical politics in S.E. Asia 329.959

330 ECONOMICS

The science of production, distribution and consumption of monetary and material wealth

.6 Commerce
.61 Internal commerce, domestic trade
.62 International commerce, foreign trade
.6206 International economic organisations and trade agreements, eg., Common Market, EFTA, GATT
.67 Tariff policy
For customs, taxes, see 351.72
.9 Economic history and geography
Add 'Areas' notation -1-9 from Table 2 to base number 330.9, eg., economic history of Great Britain, 330.941; economic geography of desert regions, 330.915
If preferred class general economic history in 909.33; economic history of specific countries in 930-999; economic geography of specific countries in 914-919

331 ECONOMICS OF LABOUR

Work, wages, working conditions

.1 Labour force and market

Composition, size, quality of labour force; types of employment; unemployment

.8 Trade unions

Labour movements, guilds

.89 Labour relations

Strikes, arbitration and other labour/management relations

332 FINANCIAL ECONOMICS

.1 Banks and banking

.4 Money

Including barter

.6 Investment finance

.7 Credit

Including hire purchase

333 LAND ECONOMICS

.1 Public control of land

333.7-333.9 UTILISATION OF SPECIFIC NATURAL RESOURCES

.7 Land utilisation

Conservation and use of forest, agricultural, urban and recreational land

Including National Parks

Class here comprehensive works on the utilisation of specific natural or power resources

For general works on conservation and pollution see 304.2; wild life reserves, 333.9; soil conservation, 631.4

It is optional to class here town and country planning: prefer 711

.8 Utilisation of subsurface (mineral) resources

.9 Utilisation of other natural resources

Conservation and use of water, shorelands, submerged lands and tidelands; air space; biological resources

Including wildlife reserves

Class here interdisciplinary works on water

If preferred class wild life reserves with specific forms of wild life, using the standard subdivision -074 from Table 1, eg., wild bird reserves, 598.074

For zoos, see 591.074

.906 Organisations concerned with conservation

eg., World Wild Life Fund, RSPB

If preferred class with specific aspect, using the standard subdivision -06 from Table 1, eg., RSPB 598.06

338 ECONOMICS OF PRODUCTION

Making economic goods and services available for the satisfaction of human wants through extraction, manufacture, transportation, storage and exchange

Including general works on factories and factory life and on agriculture related to industry

338.09 History of Production

Industrial history, industrial archaeology
Including general works on the industrial revolution
If preferred class industrial archaeology in 609; industrial history in 609

.1 Specific kinds of industries

It is optional, for the purpose of economic study, to class here specific kinds of industries: prefer Technology class 600-699

.9 Production programmes and policies

Control, subsidies, government grants, monopolies, nationalisation, industrial espionage

.91 International cartels

339 NATIONAL INCOME

Including factors affecting national income - economic depression, inflation; standards of living; the consumer society
Class here general works on poverty
For the 'Third World', developed and underdeveloped countries, see 327.2

340 LAW

Courts and justice

341 INTERNATIONAL LAW

342 NATIONAL LAW

Including constitutional and administrative law
Class here material dealing with the nature of government: its structure and constitutional base
For government activity, see 351

.2 The constitution
.4 The structure of government

343 PUBLIC LAW

Including the law of public property, public finance, regulation of industry, control of public (nationalised) industries, consumer protection
For 'law and order', see 351.74
For domestic trade, see 330.61

344 SOCIAL LAW

Including legal aspect of social welfare ('welfare state'), public order; censorship
For social and community work, see 361; social problems and disorders, 303.6 (sociological aspects) or 362 (welfare aspects); social services, 363

346 PRIVATE LAW

Including marriage, divorce; guardianship, inheritance; mortgages, bankruptcy
For sociological aspects of marriage, divorce, see 306.8

348 STATUTES

350 PUBLIC ADMINISTRATION

The organisation and management of government departments
Class individual departments with the appropriate subject, eg., education, 370
For business management and administration, see 658

350.8** Public services Public utilities

Class here public services, nationally or regionally organised but not directly controlled by central or local government authorities

.81** Water supply

Sources, storage, conservation, distribution, treatment; technology of pollution

For social and general aspects of water pollution, see 333.9

.82** Electricity supply industry

Class here general works on electrical supply

It is optional to class here generation of electricity, prefer 621.31

.83** Gas supply industry

Class here general works on gas supply industry including coal-gas, natural gas

For coal-gas technology, see 665; natural gas technology, 622

351 CENTRAL GOVERNMENT

Including parliamentary law

Class here material related to the activity of government

For the nature of government, see 342

If preferred class in 328

.09 Geographical treatment

Use 351 for central government of own country. For central government of other specific countries add 'Areas' notation -4-9 from Table 2 to base number 351.09, eg., central government of United States, 351.0973

.4 Government work force

Civil service

.7 Central government administrative activities and services

.72 Public finance

Including income tax, customs and excise, VAT, 'the budget'

.74 Public order

Police services; prisons and other penal institutions; crime investigation and prevention, 'law and order'

.75 Public safety

Civil defence

.76 Activities and services related to public morals and health

Control of drugs, alcohol, prostitution, gambling; control of pernicious diseases, quarantine regulations

.8 Central government regulation of social and economic life of the country

Including census; price controls, consumer protection, regulation of trade; regional development; environmental protection through control of industry; labour and employment regulations; regulation of health and hospital services; regulation of public utilities and transport

For civil rights, see 323.4; legal aspects of welfare state, 344; general works on welfare state, 360

.9 Malfunctioning of government, Ombudsman

352 LOCAL GOVERNMENT

Class here general works on local government and works on former units of local government, eg., shires, boroughs, parishes

352.007 Units of local government

Class here British local government reorganisation and modern units

.09 Geographical treatment

Use 352 for local government of own country. For local government of other specific countries add 'Areas' notation -4-9 from Table 2 to base number 352.09, eg., local government in United States, 352.0973

.1 Local government administrative activities and services

.12 Finance

Including the 'rates' system

.3 Public safety services

Fire service

For fire safety, see 363.36

.4 Public health services

Medical officers of health, health visitors; public pest control

.6 Environmental sanitation

.62 Sewage disposal and treatment

Use only for sewage disposal and treatment as a local government service

It is optional to class here general works on sewage disposal and treatment: prefer 628.2

.63 Waste and refuse collection

.7 Public works and housing

.73 Parks and recreation facilities

.74 Highway department services

It is optional to class here street lighting: prefer 628.9

For road construction, see 625.7; road transport, 388.3; bridge construction, 624.2

.75 Housing

Council housing

.9 Other local government administrative activities and services

eg., weights and measures, cultural activities and services, libraries

355 MILITARY ART AND SCIENCE

For military engineering; see 623

.02 War and warfare

Including battles and sieges

It is optional to class here specific wars, battles and sieges: prefer 940-999

For civil war, see 303.64

.1 Military uniforms and customs

.2** Knights and armour

.3 Espionage, spies

356 LAND FORCES AND LAND WARFARE

Including commandos and guerillas

358 AIR FORCES AND AIR WARFARE

Including land to air forces, anti-aircraft artillery: guided missiles; The Royal Air Force

For aeronautics, see 629.1; civil air transport, 389

359 SEA FORCES AND SEA WARFARE

Including the Navy

For marine engineering, see 623; transport by sea, 387

.9 Coastguards

If preferred class in 387.1

360 SOCIAL WELFARE, THE 'WELFARE STATE'

361 SOCIAL AND COMMUNITY WORK

.07 Awards for community work

eg., Duke of Edinburgh award

.5 Organised welfare and community work

.52 Privately sponsored
.522 By religious welfare organisations
.523 By independent welfare organisations
eg., Oxfam, Shelter, Help the Aged, War on Want

.53 International welfare associations

eg., International Red Cross

362 SPECIFIC SOCIAL WELFARE PROBLEMS AND SERVICES

.1 Problems of and services to specific kinds of people
.12 The old
.13 The young
Including adolescence and its problems
Class here juvenile delinquency
.17 The handicapped and disabled
Including the physically handicapped, the blind, the deaf
.18 Problem families
Including one parent families, unmarried mothers
.2 Poverty
The poor, deprivation
Including urban aid schemes
.3 Illness and disease
Public health
Including the incidence, distribution and control of disease; specific control measures, isolation, quarantine, immunisation, notifiable diseases
.4 Mental and emotional disorder
.5 Addictions

Drugs, alcoholism, gambling
For medical aspects of addiction, see 613.8

.8 Disasters

.88 Disaster relief
.89 Specific kinds of disaster
Class here causes, extent, distribution, severity, incidence, effects, control, prevention of specific kinds of disasters
.892 Disasters caused by natural conditions
eg., hurricanes, tornadoes, floods, famine
.895 Disasters caused by human activity
eg., wars, nuclear explosions

363 OTHER SOCIAL PROBLEMS AND SERVICES

.3 Public safety
Accidents and their prevention
Including first aid
.32 Road safety
Class transport accidents with appropriate transport type, eg., air crashes 389
.33** Water safety
Lifeboat service, safety in water

.36 Fire safety
For fire service, see 352.3;
.4 Pollution as a social problem
.44 Noise pollution

364 CRIMINOLOGY

For police work, crime investigation and prevention, prisons, see 351.74

.1 Criminals and outlaws

For juvenile delinquency, see 362.13

.13 Smugglers

.15 Highwaymen

.16 Pirates

Including modern piracy (hijacking)

368 INSURANCE

369 ASSOCIATIONS AND SOCIETIES

Guides, Scouts and related organisations, eg., youth clubs

370 EDUCATION

Including administration, organisation, planning of primary, secondary, further education; training of teachers

.09 History of Education

371 TEACHING

.3 Methods of instruction and study

Class teaching aids for specific subjects with the subject, using 'Standard subdivisions' notation -07 from Table 1, eg., teaching aids for mathematics, 510.7
Alternatively, if it is preferred to gather teaching aids together for a staff library, it is optional to class here all teaching aids and divide as 000-999, eg., teaching aids for mathematics, 371.351: prefer direction above

.33 Teaching materials

Including audio-visual materials, closed-circuit television, programmed texts

.4 Guidance and counselling

Class here careers guidance and materials dividing as 000-990, eg., careers material on social work, 371.436

375 CURRICULUM

378 HIGHER EDUCATION

Universities, Polytechnics, further education
Class here guides to further education

380 COMMUNICATIONS, TRANSPORT

.3 General works on communication services

.5 General works on transport

Class here interdisciplinary works on movement

383-384 COMMUNICATION SERVICES

383 POSTAL COMMUNICATION

For philately, see 790.136

.09 Historical and geographical treatment

384 TELECOMMUNICATIONS

Including recordings, visual signalling, alarms, warning systems

.1 Telegraphy

Morse and other code telegraphy
Class semaphore in 384

.2 Telephony

.5 Wireless communication

Including radiotelegraphy, radiotelephony
For radio and television broadcasting, see 791.4; closed circuit television, 371.33; radio and television and telephone engineering, 621.38

385-389 TRANSPORT SERVICES

385 RAIL TRANSPORT

It is optional to class here railway engineering: prefer 625.1, keeping 385 for commercial and social aspects

The following subdivisions should be used only if all materials on railways are to be classed here

.09 Historical treatment

.1 Personnel

.2 Locomotives and rolling stock

.3 Track and associated aspects

Including signals, tunnels, bridges

.4 Buildings associated with rail transport

Including stations, trainsheds

385.5-385.9 Types of rail systems

.5 Narrow gauge

.6 Underground

.7 Monorail

386 INLAND WATERWAY TRANSPORT

Class here comprehensive works on water transport
It is optional to class here engineering of inland waterway craft: prefer 623.82; hydraulic engineering related to inland waterways: prefer 627, keeping 386 for commercial and social aspects

The following subdivisions should be used only if all materials on inland waterways are to be classed here

.09 Historical treatment

.1 Personnel

.2 Craft

Ships, boats, barges

.4 Buildings associated with water transport

386.5-386.9 Types of inland waterway systems

.5 Rivers

.6 Canals

Including locks

.7 Lakes

387 SEA TRANSPORT

Class navigation in 527
It is optional to class here engineering of sea-going craft: prefer 623.82, keeping 387 for commercial and social aspects

The following subdivisions should be used only if all materials on sea transport are to be classed here

.09 Historical treatment

.1 Personnel

It is optional to class here coastguards: prefer 359.9

.2 Craft

Ships, submarines, hovercraft
Class underwater exploration craft in 387.5

.4 Buildings associated with sea transport

Docks, harbours, passenger terminals, lighthouses

387.5-387.7 Types of sea transport

.5 Underwater

Including underwater exploration
Class here craft associated with underwater exploration, eg., diving bells, bathyscaphes
For underwater salvage work, see 627.7; underwater exploration for buried treasure, shipwrecks, 910.4

.6 Marine services, Merchant Navy

For naval defence forces, see 359

.7 Hovercraft services

388 LAND TRANSPORT (except railways)

It is optional to class here road engineering: prefer 625.7; vehicle engineering: prefer 629.2, keeping 388 for commercial and social aspects

The following subdivisions should be used only if all materials on land transport are to be classed here

.09 Historical treatment

.1 Personnel

.2 Vehicles

Description, history, development
Including trams, 'buses, cars, bicycles, early forms of vehicular transport, eg., stagecoaches

.3 Roads and highways

Decription, history, development, classification
Including road signs; traffic control

.4 Buildings associated with road transport

eg., garages

389 AIR TRANSPORT: SPACE TRANSPORT

It is optional to class here aeronautical engineering prefer 629.1, keeping 389 for commercial and social aspects

The following subdivisions should be used only if all materials on air transport are to be classed here

389.09 Historical treatment

.1 Personnel

.2 Aircraft

For military aircraft, see 358.4

.3 Air space, Air routes

.4 Buildings associated with air transport

Airports and landing fields, heliports

389.5-389.8 SPACE TRANSPORT

It is optional to class here astronautics, space engineering: prefer 629.4, keeping 389.5 for commercial and social aspects

Class general works on space exploration and the geography of space in 910.919

The following subdivisions should be used only if all materials on space transport are to be classed here

.5 Spacemen

.6 Spacecraft

.8 Buildings associated with space travel

Launching pads

390 CUSTOMS AND FOLKLORE

394 PUBLIC AND SOCIAL CUSTOMS

Including public festivals, fairs, ceremonial customs

.2 Special occasions, holidays

398 FOLKLORE

It is optional to class here mythology: prefer 290

If the option is taken up, separate different mythologies by adding 'Area' notation for the ancient world (Tables 1 and 2) to the base number 398, eg., Indian mythology 398.0934

.2 Legends

Including tales of animals and birds

For ancient religious beliefs, mythology, see 290

If it is desired to differentiate legends by country divide as directed under 398 using 398.2 as base number

.21 Folk tales and fables

Including traditional and modern fairy tales

If preferred class fairy tales with fiction

.22 Legendary heroes

Narratives based on tradition, with or without factual foundation

Including King Arthur, Charlemagne, Robin Hood

.23 Legendary places

eg., Camelot

.3 Traditional beliefs, customs, superstitions

.32 Haunted places, ghosts

.8 Nursery rhymes and street songs

.9 Proverbs

LANGUAGE

400 LANGUAGE

Where required fuller division of this schedule is created by the application of Table 4 'Subdivisions of individual languages'

For the literature of these languages, see 800

410 LINGUISTICS

411 NOTATION

Alphabets, ideographs, cuneiform writings, phonetics: braille

419 DEAF AND DUMB LANGUAGE

420-490 SPECIFIC LANGUAGES

Under each language identified by *, add to the designated base number the 'Subdivisions of individual languages' notation -01-8 from Table 4

420 *ENGLISH LANGUAGE

Base number for English 42

429 ANGLO-SAXON (OLD ENGLISH)

430 *GERMAN LANGUAGES

Base number for German 43

439 OTHER GERMANIC LANGUAGES

.3 *Dutch, Flemish, Afrikaans

Base number for Dutch 439.3

.7 *Swedish

Base number for Swedish 439.7

.8 *Danish

Base number for Danish 439.8

.82 *Norwegian

Base number for Norwegian 439.82

440 *FRENCH LANGUAGE

Base number for French 44

450 *ITALIAN LANGUAGE

Base number for Italian 45

460 *SPANISH LANGUAGE

Base number for Spanish 46

469 *PORTUGUESE LANGUAGE

Base number for Portuguese 469

470 ITALIC LANGUAGES *LATIN

Base number for Latin 47

480 HELLENIC LANGUAGES *CLASSICAL GREEK

Base number for Classical Greek 48

Class here comprehensive works on Classical languages

489 *MODERN GREEK

Base number for Modern Greek 489

490 OTHER LANGUAGES

491 INDO-EUROPEAN (INDO-ARYAN) AND CELTIC LANGUAGES

.4 Indian languages

.42 Punjabi (Panjabi)

.43 Hindi

.439 Urdu

.44 Bengali

.45 Gujarati

.6 Celtic languages

Including *Welsh, Erse, Gaelic, Cornish

Base number for Celtic languages 491.6

.7 East Slavic languages

Including *Russian

Base number for Russian 491.7

.8 Other slavic languages

Including Polish

492 AFRO-ASIATIC (HAMITO-SEMITIC) LANGUAGES

.4 *Hebrew

Base number for Hebrew 492.4

.7 *Arabic

Base number for Arabic 492.7

494 URAL-ALTAIC LANGUAGES

Including *Finnish

Base number for Finnish 494

495 SINO-TIBETAN LANGUAGES AND LANGUAGES OF SOUTH-EAST ASIA

.1 *Chinese

Base number for Chinese 495.1

.6 *Japanese

Base number for Japanese 495.6

496 AFRICAN LANGUAGES

Including Hausa and languages of north west Africa

.3 Bantu languages

Including Swahili

499 LANGUAGES OF THE REST OF THE WORLD

Including artificial languages, eg., *Esperanto

Base number for Esperanto 499

For deaf and dumb language, see 419; for Braille see 411

PURE SCIENCES

500 PURE SCIENCES

Use 501-509 for standard subdivisions (Table 1) eg.,

Scientific apparatus	502.8
Scientific dictionaries	503
Scientific organisations	506
History of science	509

510 MATHEMATICS

Including weights and measures

511 GENERALITIES

Including mathematical logic, boolean algebra, graph theory, mathematical models, numerical analysis

512 ALGEBRA

513 ARITHMETIC

Including logarithms, permutation, numeration systems, eg., binary, decimal; ready reckoners

514 TOPOLOGY

515 ANALYSIS AND CALCULUS

516 GEOMETRY

Including euclidian and non-euclidian geometry, planes, solids, vectors; trigonometry

519 PROBABILITY AND APPLIED MATHEMATICS

.4 Computer mathematics, coding theory

For computer engineering, see 621.38

It is optional to class here data processing and use of computers, prefer 001.6

.5 Statistical mathematics

520 ASTRONOMY AND ALLIED SCIENCES

For astrology, see 133.5

521 THEORETICAL ASTRONOMY

Including specific theories, eg., quasar, pulsar, universal gravitation, orbits

522 PRACTICAL ASTRONOMY

Including techniques, apparatus, materials, equipment, eg., observatories, astronomical photography, telescopes, and other astronomical equipment; radio and radar astronomy

523 DESCRIPTIVE ASTRONOMY

.007 Museums and exhibits; planetariums

.01 Astrophysics

.1 Origin, development, structure, destiny of the universe

Including stars, nebulae, interstellar matter, galaxies, eg., Milky Way

.2 Solar system

523.3-523.7 Specific parts of the solar system

.3 Moon

.4 Planets

523.5 Meteors
.6 Comets
.7 Sun

525 EARTH (ASTRONOMICAL GEOGRAPHY)

Including seasons and tides

526 MATHEMATICAL GEOGRAPHY; SURVEYING

Including geodesy (earth's size and shape)
.8 Cartography

Map-making, reading, projection
.9 Surveying

Boundary, topographic, hydrographic surveying
Including aerial and terrestrial photogrammetry (map-making from aerial photographs)

527 NAVIGATION

Determination of geographic position and direction from observation of celestial bodies
For orienteering, see 796.5
If preferred class navigation in 797.1

529 TIME (CHRONOLOGY)

Intervals of time, calendars, horology (finding and measuring time)
Class here ancient and primitive devices for measuring time, eg., sundials, water clocks
For watch and clock making, see 681; philosophy of time, 115

530 PHYSICS

Including relativity, quantum, kinetic theories, states of matter, anti-matter

531 GENERAL MECHANICS
Including energy, gravity, mass: simple machines, eg., levers, kinematics
.2 Mechanics of solids
Including the properties of solids

532 MECHANICS OF FLUIDS

Hydromechanics, properties of fluids
Comprehensive works on mechanics of liquids and gases
For mechanics of gases only, see 533

533 MECHANICS OF GASES

Including properties of gases, kinetic theory of gases, vacuums and vacuum production, aeromechanics

534 SOUND AND RELATED VIBRATIONS

Including characteristics, eg., frequency, pitch, noise; generation, propagation (transmission), measurement, analysis, synthesis of sound; acoustics
.5 Vibrations related to sound
Subsonic, ultrasonic vibrations

535 OPTICS

Including microscopes, other optical instruments; theories; physical and geometrical optics, optical and paraphotic spectroscopy; spectral regions, eg., visible light
.6 Colour

536 HEAT

Theories; transmission (heat transfer), heat effects, temperature, thermodynamics, change of state, eg., solid to gas
For heating systems, see 690

537 ELECTRICITY AND ELECTRONICS

.1 Theories
.2 Electrostatics
.5 Electronics
Including radio waves, microwaves, electric and ion optics
.6 Electric currents and thermo-electricity
For electrical engineering, see 621.3

538 MAGNETISM

Magnets, magnetic materials and phenomena

539 MODERN PHYSICS

Molecular, atomic, nuclear physics
.2 Radiation (radiant engergy)
.7 Atomic and nuclear physics
Nuclear structure, detection and measurement of particles and radiation, x-rays, gamma-rays, cosmic-rays

540 CHEMISTRY AND ALLIED SCIENCES

For chemical technology, see 660

541 PHYSICAL AND THEORETICAL CHEMISTRY

Molecular and atomic structure

542 LABORATORIES, APPARATUS, EQUIPMENT
Class here general procedures, guides to the manipulation of equipment

543 ANALYTICAL CHEMISTRY

546 INORGANIC CHEMISTRY
Chemistry of the elements of inorganic compounds and mixtures (including water)
For interdisciplinary works on water, see 333.9

547 ORGANIC CHEMISTRY
General, physical, theoretical, analytical chemistry of carbon compounds, eg., vitamins, sugars, petroleum, rubber, dyes
For bio-chemistry, see 574.1; industrial chemistry, 660-669

548 CRYSTALLOGRAPHY
Study of structure and properties of crystals

549 MINERALOGY

Occurrence, description, identification, classification of naturally occurring elements and compounds formed by inorganic processes
For mining, see 622; geology, 550
.9 Geographical distribution of minerals
Add 'areas' notation -1-9 from Table 2 to base number 549.9

550 EARTH SCIENCES

Class here geology
For physical geography, see 910

551 **PHYSICAL GEOLOGY AND METEOROLOGY**

.1 Structure and properties of the earth

.2 Plutonic phenomena

Volcanoes, earthquakes and allied phenomena, use of seismic waves

.3 Surface processes and their agents

Weathering, erosion, deposition; transportation by ice, water, wind; sedimentation; glaciation and work of ice, icebergs

Class here interdisciplinary works on ice

.4 Geomorphology

Origin, development and transformation of topograph features; oceanography

Class here topographic description, mountains, valleys, etc

.5 Meteorology

Wind systems; atmospheric pressure; atmospheric formations, disturbances (hurricanes, tornadoes, storms, lightning) atmospheric optics (mirages, rainbows)

.6 Climate and weather

Weather forecasting

.7 Stratigraphy

Historical geology

.8 Structural geology

Form, position, deformation of rocks, eg., stratification, joints, cleavage, synclines, antisynclines, faults, folds, veins, dykes, laccoliths, sills, outcrops, strikes

552 ROCKS (PETROLOGY)

Origin, properties, composition, analysis, structure of solid materials with no fixed chemical structure

Including lithology

For minerals (solid materials with a fixed chemical structure) see 549

553 ECONOMIC GEOLOGY

Quantitative occurrence and distribution of geologic materials treated from an economic viewpoint, eg., coal, petroleum, metals, marbles, clays, salts, sulphur, soils, water, gems and precious stones

It is optional to class here interdisciplinary works on water: prefer 333.9

For birthstones, see 133.5

554-559 REGIONAL GEOLOGY

Add 'Areas' notation -4-9 from Table 2 to base number 55, eg., Geology of the East Midlands of England, 554.25

560 **PALAEONTOLOGY, PALAEOZOOLOGY**

Study of fossil plants and animals

Class here general works on prehistoric life

For prehistoric man, see 573

561 PREHISTORIC PLANTS

566 PREHISTORIC ANIMAL LIFE

567.9 PREHISTORIC REPTILES

.91 DINOSAURS

568 PREHISTORIC BIRDS

569 PREHISTORIC MAMMALS

For prehistoric man, see 573

572 HUMAN RACES (ANTHROPOLOGY)

Origin, physical characteristics
For primitive tribes and social anthropology, see 306 historical anthropology (archaeology), 909.9

.9 Distribution of human races (Ethnography)
Add 'Areas' notation -1-9 from Table 2 to base number 572.9, eg., Races of Africa 572.96

573 PHYSICAL ANTHROPOLOGY

Including prehistoric man; environmental effects on physique and pigmentation

574 BIOLOGY

Class here general nature study

.06 *It is optional to class here organisations concerned with the conservation of wild life in general: prefer 333.906*

.07 Field study

Including nature trails

.074 Museums and vivaria
It is optional to class here general wild life reserves; prefer 333.9

.1 Physiology and anatomy

.191 Biophysics

.192 Biochemistry

.3 Growth and development
Including the young of genera and species

.5 Ecology

Interrelations of organisms to environment and to each other
Class here general nature study related to specific seasons
For human ecology, see 304.2; comprehensive works on pollution and conservation, 304.2

.6 Economic biology

Organisms beneficial and deleterious to man's interests, eg., pests
For agriculture, see 630; diseases and medicine, 610; bacteria, 586

.8 Molecular biology

.9 Historical and geographical treatment
Add 'Areas' notation -3-9 from Table 2 to base number 574.9

.91** Zonal treatment
Divide as -1 from Table 2, eg., biology of grasslands 574.915

.92 Hydrographic biology

For study of fishes, see 597; study of plants, 580

.921 Marine biology

Life of sea and tidal areas; aquaria of marine life
Class tropical fish aquaria kept as a hobby in 790.134

.929 Freshwater biology

Life of ponds and rivers; aquaria of such life

.94 Regional treatment
Divide as -4-9 from Table 2, eg., biology of Polar regions 574.998

575 **ORGANIC EVOLUTION AND GENETICS**

.01 Theories of evolution

Class interdisciplinary works on evolution in 215

.1 Genetics

576 MICROBIOLOGY

578 MICROSCOPY

Slide preparation; description and use of microscopes

Class comprehensive works on microscopes in 502.8

579 **COLLECTION AND PRESERVATION OF BIOLOGICAL SPECIMENS**

For entomology as a hobby, see 790.134

580 BOTANICAL SCIENCES

581 **BOTANY**

Divide as 574

582 **SEED BEARING PLANTS**

Shrubs, vines, herbaceous plants

For cultivation of garden plants, see 635

.16 Trees

583 **FLOWERING PLANTS**

Including grasses

For cultivation of garden plants, trees and shrubs, see 635

.3 Roses

.4 Cacti

.6 Heathers

586 **SEEDLESS PLANTS**

Including ferns, fungi, lichens, mosses, bacteria

588 **MOSSES**

589 **ALGAE, FUNGI, LICHENS**

590 ZOOLOGICAL SCIENCES

591 **ZOOLOGY**

Divide as 574

592-599 SPECIFIC ANIMALS AND GROUPS OF ANIMALS

592 **INVERTEBRATES**

593 PROTISTA

Including corals, hydra, jellyfish, sea-cucumbers, sea urchins, sponges, starfish

.3 Crustaceans

Crabs, lobsters, prawns

594 MOLLUSCS (SHELLFISH)

Including clams, cockles, mussels, octopus, oysters, slugs, snails

For oyster beds (oyster farming), see 639.3; shell collecting as a hobby, 790.138; handicraft work in shells, 745.55

595 **OTHER INVERTEBRATES**

Spiders, worms

For silkworm culture, see 638

595.7 Insects

Including bees, beetles, butterflies and moths, caterpillars
For beekeeping, see 638; entomology as a hobby, 790.134

596 VERTEBRATES

597 FISHES, AMPHIBIANS AND REPTILES
For sea-shore life, see 574.921; pond and river life, 574.929; aquaria as a hobby, 790.135; fishing industry, 639; fish farming, 639.3; fishing as a sport, 799.1

.6 AMPHIBIANS
Frogs, newts, salamanders, toads

.9 REPTILES

.92 Tortoises, turtles
.95 Lizards
.96 Snakes
.98 Alligators, crocodiles

598 BIRDS

Class here general works on ornithology
For domesticated birds (farm birds), see 636.5; birds as pets, 636.61; birds and sport - pigeon racing, 798.8; game shooting, 799.2

.04 Rare, vanishing, extinct birds

.06 *It is optional to class here organisations concerned with the conservation and protection of birds: prefer 333.906*

.07 Bird watching

.074 Bird museums and aviaries
It is optional to class here wild bird reserves and sanctuaries: prefer 333.9

.2 Specific aspects of bird study

Divide as 574.1 - 574.6, eg., Bird ecology, 598.25

.29 Geographical treatment

Add 'Areas' notation -4-9 from Table 2 to base number 598.29, eg., British birds, 598.2941; South African birds, 598.2968

598.3 - 598.9 TYPES OF BIRDS

.3 Sea, shore and estuarine birds
.4 Freshwater birds; waterfowl
.5 Land birds in general

Class here zonal treatment of birds, eg., general works on birds of temperate lands or tropical birds, using 'Areas' notation -11-15 from Table 2 to obtain division, eg., mountain birds, 598.514
For tropical birds as a hobby, see 636.61

598.6 Heath and moorland birds

Including game birds

.8 Common land birds

Including garden birds

.9 Birds of prey

599 MAMMALS

For domesticated animals, see 636; animals as pets, 636.6; animals in danger of extinction, 333.9

.2 Marsupials

Mammals which carry newly born young in an abdominal pouch, eg., kangaroos, koala bears, wallabies

.3 Unguiculata

Mammals retaining some prehistoric characteristics, eg., armadillos, bats, hedgehogs

See also Primates

.32 Rabbits

.33 Rodents

Hamsters, mice, rats

.34 Beavers, guinea pigs, squirrels

.5 Marine animals

Dolphins, porpoises, seals, sea lions, walrus, whales

.6 Elephants

.7 Hooved animals

.71 Asses, horses, zebras

.72 Rhinoceros

.73 Ruminants

Antelopes, camels, dromedaries, gazelles, giraffes, moose, pigs, reindeer

.735 Bovine animals

Bison, buffalo, cattle, goats, oxen, sheep

.74 Carnivores

Bears, foxes, hyenas, tigers, wolves

.8 Primates

Apes, baboons, gorillas, monkeys

.9 Man

Use this number only for biological study of man

Class anthropological study of man in 573; specific studies of human anatomy and physiology in 611

TECHNOLOGY (APPLIED SCIENCES)

600 TECHNOLOGY (APPLIED SCIENCES)

For pure sciences, see 500
If preferred class types of industry in 338.1

604 GENERAL TECHNIQUES
Technical drawing
Engineering, mechanical, architectural drawing

608 INVENTIONS

Including patents

609 HISTORY OF APPLIED SCIENCES
It is optional to class here industrial history: prefer 338.09; industrial archaeology: prefer 338.09

610 MEDICAL SCIENCE

Including medical and hospital treatment; nursing; care of the sick and infirm

611 HUMAN ANATOMY

612 HUMAN PHYSIOLOGY

Class here comprehensive works on human anatomy and physiology

.6 Maturation (growing up); reproduction

For social aspects of growing-up and adolescence, see 305.2; social problems of growing up, 362.13; relations of the sexes, sex education, 306.7

613 GENERAL AND PERSONAL HYGIENE

Including personal cleanliness and clothing
It is optional to class here personal grooming: prefer 646.7
If preferred class general works on personal hygiene, dietetics and birth control in 646.7

.2 Dietetics, nutrition
Including slimming
If preferred class slimming in 646.7

.6 Self preservation

Including techniques of survival in accidents and unfavourable circumstances such as natural disasters, shipwreck, etc
For disaster refief, see 363.8; self-defence involving combat, 796.8

.7 Physical fitness

.8 Addictions and health
Addictive use of narcotics, alcohol, tobacco, drugs and poisons
For therapeutic use of drugs, see 615; social aspects of addiction, 362.5; criminal aspects, 351.74; government activity to control drugs, alcohol, 351.76

.9 Birth control and sex hygiene
Including family planning
It is optional to class here sex education: prefer 306.7; venereal disease: prefer 616.6
If preferred class birth control and sex hygiene in 646.7

615 PHARMACOLOGY AND THERAPEUTICS

Use of drugs and therapeutic systems in healing

.9 Poisons

616 DISEASES

.1 Heart diseases

.2 Respiratory diseases

.3 Digestive diseases

.4 Diseases of the blood

.5 Diseases of hair, skin and nails

.6 Urogenital diseases

Including veneral diseases

.7 Musculoskeletal diseases

.8 Diseases of the nervous system, mental and emotional disorders

.9 Other diseases

617 SURGERY AND RELATED TOPICS

.6 Dentistry

.7 Opthalmology (diseases of the eyes)

.8 Otology and Audiology (diseases of the ears)

618 OTHER BRANCHES OF MEDICINE

.1 Gynaecology and obstetrics

Diseases related to the reproductive proccesses in women; childbirth and pregnancy

.9 Paediatrics and geriatrics

Diseases and treatment of the young and old

620 ENGINEERING

Class here general, comprehensive works on engineering

If preferred class engineering related to various types of transport with the appropriate transport in 380-389

For a specific branch of engineering see the branch, eg., heating engineering, 690

621 MECHANICAL ENGINEERING (APPLIED PHYSICS)

Mechanical, hydraulic, electrical, electronic, thermo, light, nuclear engineering

.1 Steam engineering

Engines, boilers, steam generation and transmission

.2 Hydraulic-power techniques

Water-wheels, hydraulic pumps, rams

.3 Electrical engineering

For theory of electricity, see 537.1

.31 Electric power: generation, storage, transmission

Including hydro-electricity, power stations, national grid system

For nuclear power stations, see 621.48

If preferred class power generation with power supply in 350.82

.32 Illumination and lighting

Lighting systems regardless of source, eg., floodlighting, torches, candles, oil lamps, gas lighting

.35 Electrochemical engineering

Batteries, fuel cells, storage of solar energy

.36 Optical and paraphotic engineering

Including laser technology; technical photography, radiography

.38 Electronic and communication engineering

Class here techniques of space communication

Including computer engineering

For computer mathematics, see 519.4; use of computers, 001.6

621.381 Electronic engineering

.382 Engineering of wire and cable communication

Telegraphic, telephone engineering
For telegraphic, telephone services see 384

.384 Radio and radar engineering

For radio entertainment, see 791.44

.388 Television engineering

For television entertainment, see 791.45

.389 Sound recording and reproducing systems

Gramophones and tape recorders, public address systems, language translators
For recorded music, see 789.9; educational use of gramophones and tape recorders, 371.33

.39 Household electrical engineering and appliances
If preferred class household electrical appliances in 683

.4 Heat, combustion, air and wind engineering

.43 Internal combustion engines

.47 Solar energy engineering
For storage of solar energy, see 621.35

.48 Nuclear engineering
Including nuclear reactors, by-products, nuclear generation of thermal and electric power
For nuclear physics, see 539

.7 Factory operations engineering
Including machine and machine tool engineering

622 MINING AND MINING ENGINEERING

Including prospecting, extracting coal, gold, natural gas, petroleum, salt, silver, and other minerals; quarrying, open-cast mining
For crystallography see 548; mineralogy, 549; economic geology, 553; extraction of petroleum from sea bed, 627

623 MILITARY AND NAUTICAL ENGINEERING

For forts, fortresses, see 725; castles, 728.8

.4 Ordnance (weapons)

Ballistics and gunnery; primitive weapons, eg., bows and arrows, boomerangs; side arms, eg., swords; mines; laser, thermal, ultrasonic weapons; nuclear, chemical, biological devices; non-explosive agents, eg., tear-gas
If preferred class all weapons in 355.02
For sports weapons see the appropriate sport

.6 Military transport

For general works on transport, see 380.5

.8 Naval engineering

.82 Nautical craft

Design, construction, maintenance and repair of nautical craft, including sailing craft, hand propelled craft (canoes) and towed craft (canal barges), small and medium power driven craft, merchant ships, war ships, submarines; seamanship
If preferred class engineering of nautical craft with appropriate transport division in 386 or 387
For military science, see 355; the Navy, 359; transport by sea, 387; inland waterways, 386; navigation, 527

624 CIVIL ENGINEERING

Comprehensive works on design, construction, maintenance of public building and works
Including structural engineering

.2 Engineering of bridges and tunnels

If preferred class engineering of bridges and tunnels with the appropriate transport division in 385 or 388
For local government control of bridges, see 352.74

625 ENGINEERING OF RAILWAYS AND ROADS

.1 Railway engineering

Design, construction, maintenance of permanent way and accessories, eg., signals
If preferred class with rail transport in 385.3

.2 Locomotives and rolling stock

If preferred class with rail transport in 385.2

.7 Road engineering

Surveying, design, construction of roads; road maintenance and repair; pavements; traffic control equipment
If preferred class road engineering with road transport in 388
For local government highway services, see 352.74

627 HYDRAULIC ENGINEERING

Inland waterways, harbours and ports; dams and reservoirs, other methods of flood control; land and water reclamation; drilling platforms
Class here extraction of petroleum from sea bed
For water supply engineering, see 350.81; land reclamation for agriculture, 631.6

.7 Underwater operations

Diving, dredging, salvage

628 SANITARY ENGINEERING

Large scale public works
For household sanitary engineering (plumbing), see 690

.2 Sewage engineering

Construction, maintenance of sewerage systems and sewage treatment plants; sewage treatment and disposal
If preferred class sewage engineering in 352.62

.5 Pollution and industrial sanitation engineering

Methods and equipment for treating, salvaging and re-using industrial waste materials; recycling; products from waste materials
For social and general aspects of industrial pollution, see 333.7

.6** Hazardous materials technology

Methods of extracting, manufacturing, processing, utilising, handling, transporting, storing solids liquids and gases of explosive, flammable, corrosive, radio-active, toxic or infectious nature

628.9 Municipal lighting, street lighting

If preferred class in 352.74

629 MOTOR AND AERONAUTIC ENGINEERING

.1 Aeronautics

Including science of flight, aircraft engineering
For transport by air, see 389; gliding and flying as a sport, 797.5
If preferred class aeronautical engineering with air transport in 389.2

.2 Automobile engineering

Design and construction of vehicles
Including tractors, motor cycles, bicycles
If preferred class automobile engineering with road transport in 388.2
For internal combustion engine, see 621.43; transport by road, 388; pleasure motoring (touring), 796.78; motor cycling, motor racing as a sport, 796.7

.22 Motorised vehicles for non land surfaces

eg., ocean floor vehicles, amphibious vehicles, moon cars

.3 Hovercraft

.4 Astronautics

Techniques of space flight, engineering of space craft and related equipment
If preferred class astronautics with space travel in 389.6

.41 Space flight

.43 Unmannned flights

Including satellites
Class application of satellites for a specific purpose with the subject, eg., use of satellites for weather forecasting, 551.6

.44 Auxiliary spacecraft

Space stations and laboratories

.45 Manned flight

Including selection and training of astronauts; circumterrestrial, lunar and interplanetary flights; rescue and recovery operations

.47 Astronautical engineering

Including design, construction, maintenance and repair of spacecraft and associated facilities, eg., launching pads

.8 Automatic control engineering (automation)

Including robot and computerised control

630 AGRICULTURE AND FOOD PRODUCTION

631 GENERAL AGRICULTURE

Techniques, apparatus, equipment, materials
Including farm buildings, machinery, tools, farmland
Class home food production (gardening) in 635
For dairying, see 637; food technology (food processing), 664; home processing of food, 641

.4 Soil and soil conservation

.6 Soil reclamation and drainage

.7 Irrigation and water conservation

632 PLANT INJURIES, DISEASES, PESTS

633 FIELD CROPS

634 TREE CROPS

Orchards, fruit, nuts, plantations

.9 Forestry

Afforestation, lumbering, arboreta
For lumber industry, see 674

635 HORTICULTURE, GARDENING

Including market and home gardening

.9 Floriculture (Flowers and ornamental plants)

Including nurseries
For botanical study of plants, see 580

636 ANIMAL HUSBANDRY (LIVESTOCK)

Breeding, rearing, training, care in health and sickness, veterinary medicine
Including general works on domesticated (farm) animals
For biological study of animals, see 590

.1 Horses

.2 Cows

.3 Sheep and goats

.4 Pigs

.5 Poultry

.6 Pets (domestic animals)

.61 Birds as pets, cage birds

For pigeon racing, see 798.8

.7 Dogs

.8 Cats

.9 Other animals as pets

Guinea pigs, hamsters, mice, rabbits

637 DAIRYING AND RELATED TECHNIQUES

Production, processing and marketing of all dairy products
For breeding and rearing of cattle, see 636.2; mixed farms, 631

638 INSECT CULTURE

Culture of bees, silkworms; production of honey, beeswax
For silk production, see 677; biological study of insects, 595.7; entomology as a hobby, 790.134

639 NON-DOMESTICATED ANIMALS AND PLANTS

Hunting, trapping, sealing
For hunting, shooting, fishing as sports, see 799; fish breeding as a hobby, 790.135

.2 Fishing industry, whaling

.3 Fish farming

Including oyster beds

640 HOME ECONOMICS (DOMESTIC ARTS AND SCIENCE)

Care of the household, family, person
Class here household management, household finances
For personal hygiene, see 613

640.73 Consumer education

Including guides to quality and value in products and services; organisations concerned with such education

641 FOOD AND DRINK, APPLIED NUTRITION

For food production, see 630; commercial food manufacture and processing, 664

.2 Drink

Alcoholic and non-alcoholic beverages

.4 Preservation of food

Cold storage, deep freezing, brining, pickling, use of additives

.5 Cookery

Preparation of food with or without heat

.6 Specific types of cookery

642 DINING, ENTERTAINING

Planning menus, table service and decor in the home and public eating places

Including catering for parties; etiquette of dining and entertaining

For flower arrangement, see 745.92

643 THE HOME AND ITS EQUIPMENT

Selection; purchase, rental, mortgages; location; arrangement of equipment in the home; house repair and maintenance; do-it-yourself improvements

For house building, see 690; domestic architecture, 728

645 HOUSEHOLD FURNISHINGS

Selection and execution of schemes of decoration and furnishing

Including floor coverings, wall coverings, paints and other colour schemes; hangings, curtains, drapes, shades, blinds; other accessories

For interior decoration and design, see 747; home rug making, 746.7; furniture manufacture, 684

.09** Antiques

646 CLOTHES AND PERSONAL GROOMING

Including choice and care of clothing

.09 History of clothing and costume

For stage costume, see 792, national costume, 394

.2 Sewing and related operations

.4 Dressmaking

For history of dress, see 646.09; commercial manufacture of clothing, 688; embroidery, 746.3

.6 Care of clothes

Laundering, dry cleaning

.7 Personal grooming

Including beauty culture, cleanliness, care of hair, professional hairdressing, use of wigs

If preferred class personal grooming in 613

It is optional to class here slimming: prefer 613.2; sex education: prefer 306.7; birth control and sex hygiene: prefer 613.9

647 PUBLIC HOUSEHOLDS

Hotels, motels, inns, public houses, hostels

648 HOUSEHOLD SANITATION

Laundering, housecleaning, control and eradication of household pests

649 CHILD CARE

It is optional to class here child rearing and related subjects: prefer 305.2

650 MANAGEMENT SERVICES, BUSINESS METHODS

651 OFFICE MANAGEMENT

.5 Record management

Filing systems, procedures; storage, micro-reproduction, computerisation of files

.7 Communication

Correspondence, reports, minutes and oral communication

Including handling of mail, dictation and use of dictation equipment

For data processing, see 001.6

652 PROCESSES OF WRITTEN COMMUNICATION

Guides to letter, report, technical minute writing; business correspondence; typing

For calligraphy, see 745.6

653 SHORTHAND AND SPEEDWRITING

657 ACCOUNTING AND BOOKKEEPING

658 GENERAL MANAGEMENT AND ADMINISTRATION

Principles of management; management of businesses

For public administration, see 350

.8 Management of distribution

Marketing, salesmanship; points of distribution, shops, markets, fairs, auctions; vending machines

659 ADVERTISING AND PUBLIC RELATIONS

660 CHEMICAL AND RELATED TECHNOLOGIES (CHEMICAL INDUSTRY)

661 TECHNOLOGY OF INDUSTRIAL CHEMICALS (HEAVY INDUSTRY)

Large scale production of chemicals as raw materials or reagents in the manufacture of other products

Including petroleum derivatives

For industrial gases, see 665

662 TECHNOLOGY OF EXPLOSIVES, FUELS AND RELATED PRODUCTS

Fireworks, propellants, detonators, matches; processing of coal, coke, charcoal; production of non-fuel carbons, eg., graphite, carbon-black synthetic fuels; fire fighting equipment, eg., fire extinguishers

For coal mining, see 622; petroleum and gaseous fuel processing, 665

663 BEVERAGE TECHNOLOGY

Commercial manufacture and processing of alcoholic and non-alcoholic drinks

664 FOOD TECHNOLOGY

Commercial manufacture and processing of food

Including refrigeration, canning, drying, dehydrating, smoking

For food production, see 630, home preservation and cooking, 641.4-641.7

665 TECHNOLOGY OF INDUSTRIAL OILS, FATS, WAXES AND GASES

Of animal, vegetable or mineral origin

Including petroleum, fuel gases and other industrial gases

For petroleum derivatives, see 661, extraction of petroleum, 622

666 CERAMICS AND ALLIED INDUSTRIES

Including commercial pottery making, porcelain, stoneware, earthenware, enamels, cement, glass; refractory materials, eg., asbestos; structural clay products, eg., bricks; synthetic and artificial minerals and stones; masonry additives, eg., plaster of Paris
For hand thrown pottery, see 738

667 CLEANING AND DYEING INDUSTRIES

Including manufacture of paint, pigment, varnish, ink; cleaning and bleaching of textiles, furs, leather
For home laundering, see 648; textile handicrafts, 746

668 TECHNOLOGY OF OTHER ORGANIC PRODUCTS

Including manufacture of soaps, detergents, wetting agents, glycerine, glues, perfumes, pesticides, soil conditioners and fertilisers
For man-made fibres, see 677

.4 Plastics

Class plastic based fabrics and fibres in 677

669 METALLURGY

Production and properties of metals
For mining, see 622; manufacture of metal products, 671; art metalwork, 739

.028 Metal manufacturing

Including blast-furnaces, ore smelting, foundries; hot and cold rolling; welding, soldering, brasing, riveting

.1 Manufacture of ferrous metals

.2 Manufacture of non ferrous metals

670-689 MANUFACTURES (SECONDARY INDUSTRIES)

670 PROCESSING INDUSTRIES

671 MANUFACTURE OF METAL PRODUCTS

674 LUMBER INDUSTRY

Wood and cork processing; saw-mill operations
For forestry, see 634.9; woodwork, carpentry, 684; wood carving handicrafts, 745.51; joinery 690

675 LEATHER AND FUR PROCESSING

Tanning, dressing, finishing hides; manufacture of imitation leather and furs
For trapping, see 639; art leatherwork, 745.53

676 PAPERMAKING AND RELATED PRODUCTS

Including products manufactured from pulp, eg., fibreboard and pulp by-products, eg., turpentine

677 TEXTILES

Yarns, threads, fabrics made from natural and synthetic fibres
Including commercial carpet making, rope and cord manufacture
For handweaving, see 746.1; silkworm culture, 638; dyeing and printing of textiles, 667; textile handicrafts, 746

678 RUBBER AND RELATED PRODUCTS

Natural and synthetic rubbers and products made from them
Class elastic textiles in 677

679 OTHER PRODUCTS

Including cigarette manufacture
For products from waste materials, see 628.54

680 CRAFT INDUSTRIES

681 PRECISION INSTRUMENTS

Including manufacture and repair of measuring instruments, watches, clocks, calculating machines, slide rules, optical instruments - cameras, telescopes, microscopes; printing, writing, duplicating machines and equipment; musical instruments
Class ancient and primitive devices for measuring time, eg., sundials, in 529
For general works on microscopes, see 502.8; microscopy, 578

682 BLACKSMITH AND SMALL FORGE WORK

Including wrought ironware

683 HARDWARE

Manufacture of household appliances
It is optional to class here electrical household appliances, prefer 621.39

.3 Locksmithing

.4 Gunsmithing

For military use of guns, see 355; guns for sport, 799

684 FURNITURE MAKING, WOODWORKING

Including carpentry, home handyman and other amateur workshop manuals

.09 History of funiture making

686 PRINTING AND RELATED ACTIVITIES

For book illustration, see 741.6; journalism, 070; book publishing, 070.5

.2 Printing

.3 Bookbinding

.4 Photoduplication (photocopying)

687 CLOTHING MANUFACTURE

For home dressmaking, see 646.4

688 OTHER FINAL PRODUCTS

Including jewellery manufacture
For craft jewellery, see 739.2

.7 Recreational equipment

Toys, equipment for games and sports
For model making, handicraft toys, see 745.59

690 BUILDING CONSTRUCTION

Including masonry, joinery, plumbing, painting, heating, ventilation engineering
For architecture, see 720; interior decoration and design, 747; home improvements and repair, 643

THE ARTS

700 THE ARTS

Fine, decorative, graphic, performing; entertainments, recreations, sports
For literature, see 800

703 DICTIONARIES, ENCYCLOPAEDIAS OF THE ARTS

705 PERIODICALS OF THE ARTS

708 PUBLIC AND PRIVATE COLLECTIONS

Including guide books, catalogues of specific collections and museums
For antiques, see 645.09

709 HISTORY OF THE ARTS

.01 Primitive and early art

.02 500-1400

Including early christian, byzantine, romanesque gothic

.03 1400-1600

Renaissance, classicism

.031 1600-1800

Including baroque, rococo

.032 1800-1900

Including classical revival (neoclassicism), romanticism, naturalism, impressionism, luminism, post impressionism

.04 20th Century, 1900-

Including abstract art, cubism, dadaism, surrealism
Class here modern arts
Class prehistoric art in 306
For the arts by country add 'Areas' notation -4-9 to the base number 709; for history of specific fields of the arts, see the subject, eg., history of painting, 759

710 CIVIC AND LANDSCAPE ART, PLANNING

.06 National Trust

711 TOWN AND COUNTRY PLANNING

Design of the physical environment for public welfare, convenience, pleasure on international, national, regional and local level
Including social and economic factors determining planning
If preferred class in 333.7

712 LANDSCAPE DESIGN

Including public parks and grounds; private and semi-private grounds open to the public
It is optional to class here private and semi-private buildings open to the public (historic houses): prefer 728.8
For building design, see 720; building construction, 690; private (domestic) gardening, 635

720 ARCHITECTURE

Including history and description
For specific schools and styles of architecture divide as 709
For building construction, see 690; interior design, 747

725 PUBLIC BUILDINGS

Including forts and fortresses
For castles, see 728.8
If preferred class forts and fortresses in 728.8

726 RELIGIOUS BUILDINGS

Temples, shrines, mosques; churches, cathedrals; monastic buildings
Class here graveyards, tombstones

728 RESIDENTIAL BUILDINGS

Structures designed for permanent and temporary homes; houses, flats, cottages, bungalows, houseboats

.8 Large and elaborate private dwellings

Castles, palaces, mansions, manor houses, historic houses
If preferred class specific castles, palaces historic houses open to the public in 712, or with local history in 910.9
It is optional to class here forts and fortresses: prefer 725

730-750 CREATIVE ARTS

730 SCULPTURE

The creation of three dimensional objects by carving in stone, wood or plastic material and modelling in clay or other pliable substances
Including history and description

736 CARVING AND CARVINGS

Sculpture of smaller three dimensional objects; cameos; cutting of precious and semi-precious stones
For wood carving as a handicraft, see 745.51

737 COINS, MEDALS, SEALS, SIGNETS, TALISMANS, TOKENS

For the collection of coins, medals as a hobby (numismatics), see 790.137; economic use of coins, 332.4

738 CERAMIC ARTS

Including the materials and techniques of porcelain, earthenware, pottery, enamels, mosaics, ornamental bricks, tiles
For the commercial manufacture of ceramics, see 666

739 ART METALWORK

Decorative work, other than sculpture, in common metals
For metallurgy, see 669; industrial metalwork, 671

.2 Decorative work in precious metals, metal jewellery making

740 DRAWING, DECORATIVE ARTS AND CRAFT, DESIGN

741 DRAWING, SKETCHING
For map drawing (cartography), see 526.8; technical drawing, 604.2

.6 Commercial art

745 DECORATIVE ARTS AND CRAFTS

Class interior decoration and design in 747

745.5 Handicrafts

Creative work done by hand or with aid of simple tools or machines

745.51-745.57 Handicrafts in specific materials

.51 Wood

Marquetry, ornamental woodwork wood carving

.53 Leather and other fabrics

.54 Paper

Folding, cutting, montage; origami; papier mache

.55 Shells

For collecting shells, see 790.138

.56 Metals

Including wire work, filament designs and pictures

.57 Other materials

.59 Handicraft of specific objects

eg., toys, models; mobiles, decorations for specific occasions (eg., Christmas); artificial flowers; lampshades

Class here handicrafts in composite materials

For arrangement of artificial flowers, see 745.92

.6 Calligraphy

Including artistic lettering, illumination

For illuminated manuscripts, see 090

.9 Other decorative arts

Including Filography (Pin and thread designs)

.92 Floral arts

Flower arrangement; selection and arrangement of plant material and appropriate accessories

For table decoration, see 642

746 TEXTILE ARTS AND HANDICRAFTS

For dressmaking, see 646.4; commercial textile manufacture, 677

.1 Spinning and weaving

Including textiles created by framework, eg., hairpin lace, bobbin work

.2 Raffia, rush work, basketry

.3 Needlepoint work

Tapestry, embroidery, beaded embroidery, quilting, feltcraft, collage

.4 Needlework

Knitting, crochet work, tatting, drawn thread work

.5 Beadwork

For beaded embroidery, see 746.3

.6 Fabric printing, painting, dyeing

Block and silk screen printing, resist dyeing, tie and dye, hand decoration, stencilling, batik

.7 Rugs and carpets

For commercial carpet manufacture, see 677

.9 Other textile handicrafts

Macrame

747 INTERIOR DECORATION AND DESIGN

748 **GLASS WORK**

Engraving, stained glass, ornamental glassware
For commercial glass production, see 666

750 **PAINTING AND PAINTINGS**

751 PROCESSES AND FORMS
.4 Techniques
.5 Reproduction and copying
Including forgeries
For prints and print making, see 760
.6 Care, preservation and restoration

753 SPECIFIC SUBJECTS OF PAINTING AND PAINTINGS
Abstraction, symbolism, mythology and legends, everyday life, religious figures and stories, historical events, human form, landscapes, still life, industrial scenes

759 HISTORICAL TREATMENT
For specific schools and styles not limited by country divide as 709
.9 GEOGRAPHICAL TREATMENT
Add 'Areas' notation -4-9 from Table 2 to base number 759.9
For individual painters use 759.92 plus first three letters of the subject's name if required

760-769 GRAPHIC ARTS

760 **PRINTS AND PRINT MAKING**

For commercial printing, see 686; publishing, 070.5

761 **BLOCK PRINTING**

Printing from raised surfaces
Including rubbing (brass rubbing)

763 LITHOGRAPHY

764 SILK SCREEN PRINTING

765 ENGRAVING

767 ETCHING

770 **PHOTOGRAPHY**

Including cine-photography, amateur film making
For commercial film making, cinema as entertainment, see 791.4; television and cinema newsreels and documentaries, 070; photoduplication (photocopying, xerography), 686.4

780-789 MUSIC

780 **MUSIC**

Description and appraisal of works and musicians
Class here general works about music

If desired distinguish scores, music manuscripts by prefixing 'M' to appropriate class number, eg., operatic scores M782.1

.16 Bibliographies
.2 Miscellany
.23 Music as a profession, occupation, hobby
Class here musical reminiscences

780.24 Recording of music

Gramophone records ('discs'), discographies record catalogues

.27 Scores

Including miniature scores

.7 Study and teaching

.79 Festivals, competitions, awards

.9 History of music

.92 Individual musicians

Class here biographies and critical appraisal of performers and interpreters of music only

For composers see 789

781 GENERAL PRINCIPLES

Including musical theory and structure; musical forms; musical notation

.2 Elements of music

Harmony, melody and counterpoint; tonality

.4 Performances of music

Description and critical appraisal

.5 MUSIC FOR SPECIFIC TIMES

.52 Music for specific occasions or days

Anniversaries, Sundays

.53 Music for Christmas

.54 Music for Spring, Easter

.58 Community singing

For songs, see 782.4

.59 Film, radio and television music

.6 SPECIFIC KINDS OF MUSIC

.622 Folk music

For songs, see 782.4

.623 Pop music

.626 Jazz

.65 Ballet music

.69 Patriotic music

.9 Dance music

782 VOCAL MUSIC

.1 Opera

.13 Operetta, musicals

.2 Choral music

Anthems, cantatas, oratorios and passions, spirituals

.27 Hymns

.28 Carols

If preferred class hymns and carols in 245

.3 Liturgical music

Settings of Christian liturgy; mass, requiem mass, stabat mater, credo, etc.

.4 Songs, madrigals

.7 Works for children's voices

784 ENSEMBLES OF INSTRUMENTS AND THEIR MUSIC

Class here comprehensive works on instrumental music

.2 Orchestral and instrumental ensembles and their music

Class here works for the full orchestra, eg., symphonies

.22 General orchestral works with incidental vocal part

.23 General orchestral works with solo instruments

Including concertos

784.3 Brass bands

786-788 INDIVIDUAL INSTRUMENTS AND THEIR MUSIC

786 Class here comprehensive works on musical instruments

786.2-786.5 Keyboard instruments

.2 Stringed keyboard instruments
Piano, harpsichord, virginal

.5 Organ

.55 Other keyboard instruments
Electronic organ, harmonium, accordion, concertina

.6 Mechanical instruments and devices
Barrel organ, reproducing and player pianos, piano rolls; musical boxes

.7 Electronic musical instruments
Including musique conrete

.8 Percussion instruments and their music

787 Stringed instruments and their music

788 Wind instruments and their music

.36 Recorder

.9 Individual brass band instruments
For Brass Band music, see 784.3

789 INDIVIDUAL COMPOSERS AND THEIR MUSIC
If preferred class composers generally related to a specific medium with the medium, eg., Verdi with opera at 782.1

790-799 RECREATION AND PERFORMING ARTS

790 RECREATION

.01 Philosophy and theory of recreation
Including effective use of leisure and retirement

.1 Recreational activities

.13 Hobbies

Recreational activities usually engaged in by individuals

.134 Entomology

Collection of insects particularly butterflies

.135 Home aquaria of warm and cold water fish and plants

.136 Philately

Collection of postage stamps

.137 Numismatics

Collection of coins and medals

.138 Collection of shells, pebbles and rock specimens

.139 Other collecting hobbies

Class bird-keeping as a hobby in 636.61

.15 Hobbies involving more than one person

.151 Model railways

.152 War gaming

Collection of and games played with model soldiers and military equipment

790.19 Activities and programmes for specific classes of people, eg., Youth clubs, Darby & Joan clubs, Women's guilds

791-792 PERFORMING ARTS

791 PUBLIC ENTERTAINMENT

For stage performances, see 792; musical performances, 781.4; music drama performances, 782

.3 Circuses

.4 Mass media as entertainment

.43 Motion pictures (cinema)

.44 Radio

.45 Television

For amateur film making, see 770; radio engineering, 621.384; television engineering, 621.388

.5 Miniature, toy, shadow theatres

Including puppets

.6 Pageants

Processions, illuminations (son et lumiere), parades

.8 Animal performances

Bullfighting, rodeos
For circus animal performances, see 791.3; equestrian sports and animal racing, 798

792 THEATRE

Play production, dramatic art, art of stage make-up, costume
For use of cosmetics (make-up), see 646.7; history of costume, 646.09

.09 Description, critical appraisal of specific theatres and theatre companies

For play texts and criticism see appropriate section of 800 schedule

.3 Pantomime

.8 Ballet

For ballet music, see 781.65; presentation of musical drama, 782.1

793 INDOOR GAMES AND AMUSEMENTS

For indoor games of skill, see 794; indoor games of chance, 795

.2 Party games

Including charades, quizzes

.3 Dancing

Folk, country, ballroom, square; theatrical (tap) dancing
For ballet dancing, see 792.8; national dances, 394

.7 Puzzles, mathematical games

.73 Crosswords

.8 Magic, conjuring, juggling, ventriloquism

794 INDOOR GAMES OF SKILL

.1 Chess

794.2 Draughts

.3 Darts

.6 Bowling

.7 Ball games

Billiards, snooker, table tennis

795 GAMES OF CHANCE

Class here table games, dominoes, dice, bingo; gambling and betting, probability of winning

.4 Card games

796 ATHLETICS, SPORTS, OUTDOOR GAMES

.1 Miscellaneous games

Class here comprehensive works on children's outdoor games: roller skating; kites

.3 Ball games

.32 Balls thrown or hit by hand

Volleyball, basketball, netball

For rounders, see 796.35

.33 Balls kicked

Football, rugby

.34 Raquet games

Tennis, lacrosse, squash, badminton

.35 Balls driven by club, mallet or bat

Polo, croquet, hockey, rounders

.352 Golf

.358 Cricket

.4 Athletics and gymnastics

Including trampolining

Class here Olympic Games

Class winter Olympic Games in 796.9

.5 Outdoor life

Including orienteering

.51 Walking

.52 Rock climbing, mountaineering

.525 Caving, pot-holing (speleology)

.53 Beach combing

.54 Camping

.6 Cycling

.7 Motor racing, motor cycling

.78 Pleasure touring, touring by car

.8 Combat sports

Wrestling, boxing, fencing, judo, karate, kung-fu, self defence involving combat

.9 Winter sports

Ice hockey; ice skating; skiing; tobogganing; curling

Class here winter Olympic Games

797 AQUATIC SPORTS AND AIR SPORTS

For fishing, see 799.1

.1 Sailing; surfing

It is optional to class here navigation: prefer 527

.2 Swimming and diving

Including underwater swimming; skin, scuba diving; water games, water polo

For underwater exploration, see 387.5

797.5 Air sports

Aircraft racing, flying for pleasure, stunt flying, gliding, hang-gliding, parachuting, skydiving

798 EQUESTRIAN SPORTS ANIMAL RACING

Horsemanship, ponycraft, horseracing, gymkhanas

.8 Animal racing

Greyhound, pigeon racing

799 HUNTING AND SHOOTING SPORTS

For hunting, trapping, fishing industries, see 639

.1 Fishing

.2 Hunting

Including game shooting, use of rifles, shotguns; falconry

.3 Shooting other than for game

Clay pigeon shooting, archery, target shooting

LITERATURE

Where required fuller division of this schedule is created by the application of Table 3 'Subdivisions of individual literatures'
See also the Preface section 5:4:1:b 'Alternatives for classifying literature'

800 LITERATURE

Works of literature and commentary on them
For language, see 400; literatures of individual countries, 810-899; folk literature, 398

800-809 GENERAL WORKS CONCERNED WITH LITERATURE

Add standard subdivisions -01-07 from Table 3, subdivisions of individual literatures, to base number 8; eg., general dictionaries of literature, 803

808 LITERARY COMPOSITION
.5 Public speaking
Speech training, debate, choral speaking, rhetoric

810-890 LITERATURES OF SPECIFIC LANGUAGES

Each literature identified by * may be more fully divided either according to the form (poetry, drama, etc,) or by historical period; or by both, if so required.
Full details are given in section 5:4:1:b of the preface

810 *AMERICAN LITERATURE
Including Canadian literature written in English
Base number 81

820 *ENGLISH LITERATURE
Base number 82
Works of William Shakespeare are allocated a special place at 822.3
.9 Anglo Saxon; Old English

830 *GERMAN LITERATURE
Base number 83

839 OTHER GERMANIC LITERATURES
.3 *Dutch, Flemish, Afrikaans
Base number for Dutch 839.3
.7 *Swedish
Base number 839.7
.8 *Danish
Base number 839.8
.82 *Norwegian
Base number 839.82

840 *FRENCH LITERATURE
Base number 84

850 *ITALIAN LITERATURE
Base number 85

860 *SPANISH LITERATURE
Base number 86

869 *PORTUGUESE LITERATURE
Base number 869

870 *LATIN LITERATURE
Base number 87
Including stories from the classics, eg., stories from Virgil
For myths and legends, see 292.937

880 HELLENIC LITERATURES *CLASSICAL GREEK
Base number for Classical Greek 88
Including stories from the classics, eg., stories from Homer
For myths and legends, see 292.938

889 *MODERN GREEK LITERATURE
Base number 889

890 LITERATURE OF OTHER LANGUAGES

891 INDO-EUROPEAN (INDO-ARYAN) AND CELTIC LITERATURES

.4 Indian Literatures
.42 Punjabi (Panjabi) Literature
.43 Hindi Literature
.439 Urdu Literature
.44 Bengali Literature
.45 Gujarati Literature

.6 Celtic Literature
Including *Welsh, Erse, Gaelic, Cornish
Base number for Celtic literatures 891.6
.7 East Slavic Literatures *Russian Literature
Base number for Russian 891.7
.8 Other Slavic Literatures
Including Polish Literature

892 AFRO-ASIATIC (HAMITO-SEMITIC) LITERATURES
.4 *Hebrew Literature
Base number 892.4
For biblical works, see 220
.7 *Arabic Literature
Base number 892.7

894 URAL-ALTAIC LITERATURES
Including *Finnish
Base number for Finnish 894

895 LITERATURES OF SOUTH EAST ASIA SINO-TIBETAN LITERATURES

.1 *Chinese Literature
Base number 895.1
.6 *Japanese Literature
Base number 895.6

896 AFRICAN LITERATURES
Including Hausa and literatures of north west Africa
.3 Bantu Literatures
Including Swahili

899 LITERATURES OF THE REST OF THE WORLD
Including literatures of artificial languages, eg., Esperanto
Base number for *Esperanto 899
Add 'Areas' notation -094-099 to divide by country, eg., Australian Literature 899.0994 (whether in English or native languages)

HISTORY, GEOGRAPHY, DESCRIPTION, TRAVELS, BIOGRAPHY

900 GENERAL HISTORY AND GEOGRAPHY

Narrative and analysis of events in the distant or immediate past in the life of mankind, not limited to a single subject or discipline
Class historical treatment of a specific subject with the subject, using 'Standard subdivisions' notation -09 from Table 1, eg., history of science, 509
For history of a specific region or locality, see 930-990, eg., history of Asia 950; of India, 954

901-909 GENERAL HISTORY

901 PHILOSOPHY AND THEORY OF GENERAL HISTORY

902-908 HISTORY GENERALITIES

Add 'Standard subdivisions' notation -02-06 from Table 1 to base number 9, eg., periodicals on general history, 905; historical associations, 906

909 GENERAL WORLD HISTORY

Class here general history of specific groups of people not limited by continent, country or locality, eg., world history of the Jews; general history of negroid people

.33 *It is optional to class here general economic history: prefer 330.9*

.9 Civilisation

Man's spiritual, intellectual, material situation and changes in this
Including antiquities and archaeology
It is optional to class here industrial archaeology: prefer 338.09

910-919 GEOGRAPHY, DESCRIPTION, TRAVEL

910 GENERAL GEOGRAPHY

Description and analysis of the earth's surface and man's civilisation upon it
Class here philosophy and theory of geography
For geography of a specific region, see the region, eg., geography of Europe, 914; of London, 914.21
Class geographical treatment of a specific subject with the subject, using 'Standard subdivisions' notation -09 from Table 1, eg., economic geography, 330.9; birds of Africa, 598.296

.1 Geographical treatment of specific subjects
It is optional to class here topical geography: prefer the specific subject number (with the standard subdivision notation -09 Geographical treatment added), eg., economic geography, 330.9; urban geography, 307.769
If the option is taken up add 001-899 to the base number 910.1, eg., economic geography, 910.133; urban geography 910.1307

910.21 Statistical material related to geography

.22 Illustrations and models

Class maps and charts in 912

.23 Audio-visual materials related to general geography

.25 Directories

.3 Dictionaries, encylopaedias, gazetteers

Including general works on place names

For personal names, see 929

.4 Travel and adventure, General exploration

Including accounts of voyages, travels, journeys in several parts of, or around, the world; ancient shipwrecks, buried treasure, underwater exploration; pirates' voyages

For travels, exploration, discovery in a specific place, see the place, eg., travels in France, 914.4

.406 Tourist industry

Class here general works on tourism and the travel industry

Class materials related to specific areas with the area

.5 Geographical periodicals

.6 Geographical organisations

.9 Geography of non political regions

Add 'Areas' notation -1-19 from Table 2 to base number 910.9, eg., general geography of rivers 910.9169; of deserts 910.9154

911 HISTORICAL GEOGRAPHY

Class here historical atlases

Class here materials related to the study of local history in general

Class materials related to the local history of a specific locality in 914-919, (adding 'Standard subdivision' notation -09 to the number for the locality if required)

For industrial Archaeology, see 338.09

912 ATLASES AND MAPS

For map making, cartography, see 526.8

Class Atlases of specific subjects with the subject, eg., Atlases of wild animal life, 591.9

914-919 GEOGRAPHY OF AND TRAVEL IN SPECIFIC AREAS

Add 'Areas' notation -4-9 from Table 2 to base number 91, eg., London 914.21; Azores Islands, 914.69; Canada, 917.1; South Pacific, 919.6

If preferred class in 940-999
[see also index of places]

920 BIOGRAPHY

Including autobiographies, diaries, letters, when none of these is primarily of literary, artistic or subject interest

Class here collected biography

Class single biographies in 920 plus the first three letters of the biographee's name, eg., a biography of Winston Churchill, 920 CHU

If preferred class biographies of people associated with a particular subject with the subject, adding 'Standard subdivisions' notation -092 to the number for the subject, eg., Henry Ford, 629.2092

[for alternatives for classifying biography, see Preface]

929 GENEALOGY AND HERALDRY

Including personal names, surnames, flags, family histories

For place names, see 910.3

930-990 HISTORY OF SPECIFIC AREAS

It is optional to class here general geography and travel related to specific areas of the world: prefer 914-919; economic history of specific areas of the world: prefer 330.9

For subdivision by areas add 'Areas' notation -3-9 from Table 2 to the base number 9 (adding an '0' if required to complete a three digit number), eg., general history of Europe, 940; of British Isles, 941; of Africa, 960

Then add, if required

001-008 Standard subdivisions notation from Table 1 and/or

01-09 Historical periods

[see also index of places]

930 GENERAL HISTORY OF THE ANCIENT WORLD

For antiquities and archaeology, see 909

930 THE ANCIENT WORLD to c500 AD

931 CHINA to c420 AD

932 EGYPT AND THE NILE VALLEY to c640 AD

933 PALESTINE (INCLUDING JUDEA) to c70 AD

934 INDIA to 647 AD

935 MESOPOTAMIA to c640 AD

936 EUROPE to c500 AD

Excluding Mediterranean region

.2 British Isles to c410 AD

.3 Germanic regions to c500 AD

.4 Celtic regions to c500 AD

.6 Iberian peninsula to c500 AD

937 ITALIAN PENINSULA AND ADJACENT TERRITORIES to 476 AD

Class here Roman Empire

938 GREECE to 323 AD

Class here Alexandrian Empire

939 EASTERN MEDITERRANEAN to c640 AD

Class here Phoenician and Carthaginian Empires

HISTORICAL SUBDIVISIONS FOR MAJOR COUNTRIES

For general history notation for all countries of world, see instructions under 930-990 and also index of places

940 GENERAL HISTORY OF EUROPE

From fall of Rome 476, to present day

.1 Middle ages. 476-1453

Including the Crusades

.2 Modern Europe, 1453-1914

.21 Renaissance, 1453-1517

.22 Reformation to French revolution, 1517-1789

.27 Napoleonic era, 1789-1815

.28 Nineteenth century, 1815-1914

.3 World War I, 1914-1918

Social, political, economic, diplomatic aspects; causes, results

940.4 World War I, 1914-1918

Military history; conduct of the war

.5 Twentieth century, 1918-present day

Including comprehensive works on twentieth century

.51 Post war and depression years, 1919-1939

.53 World War II, 1939-1945

Social, political, economic, diplomatic aspects; causes, results

.54 World War II, 1939-1945

Military history; conduct of the war

.55 Later twentieth century 1945-

Class here general works on post World War II period

.56** Mid-twentieth century, the 'cold war' 1945-63

.561** Modern times, 1963 onwards

Including the 'European Movement'

941 HISTORY OF BRITISH ISLES, GREAT BRITAIN, UNITED KINGDOM

For local history in general, see 911; of a specific area, see 914.1 - 914.29; history of England, 942

.01 Early history

General works on Celtic tribes and invasions of Angles, Saxons, Danes, Vikings

.06 Act of union

.07 Georgian period 1714-1837

.08 Victorian era to present day

.081 Victoria, 1837-1901

.082 Twentieth century 1901 - present day

Class here general works on twentieth century Britain

.0823** Edward VII, 1901-1910

.083 George V, 1910-1936

Class general works on World War I in 940.3

.084 Edward VIII, George VI and World War II 1936-1945

Class general works on World War II in 940.53

.085 Later twentieth century 1945-

Class here general works on post-war Britain

.086** Elizabeth II, 1952-

.1 HISTORY OF SCOTLAND

For local history, see 914.11-914.14

.101 Early history to 1057

.102 Early efforts at control by England, 1057-1314

.103 Early period of independence, 1314-1424

.104 Early Stuarts, James I-V, 1424-1542

.105 Reformation, 1542-1603

Including Mary Queen of Scots

.106 Personal union with England, 1603-1707

Including the Act of union and the reign of Anne, 1708-1714

The following notation should be used only for material related specifically to Scotland in the period after the Act of union

.107 Georgian period 1714-1837

Including the Jacobite rebellions

.108 Victorian era to present day

.1081 Victoria, 1837-1901

.1082** Edward VII, 1901-1910

.1083** George V, 1910-1936

.1084** Edward VIII and George VI, 1936-1952

.1086** Elizabeth II, 1952-

941.5 HISTORY OF IRELAND, 410-1922

.501 Early history, 410-1086
.502 Disorder and English conquest, 1087-1171
.503 Plantagenets, 1171-1399
.504 Lancaster and York, 1399-1485
.505 Tudors, 1485-1603
.506 Stuarts, 1603-1714
.507 Eighteenth century
.508 Nineteenth and twentieth centuries
Including the 'Troubles', 1916-1922

.6 HISTORY OF ULSTER
.608** Nineteenth and twentieth centuries
Class here general works on nineteenth and twentieth centuries in Northern Ireland
.6083** Northern Ireland since 1920
.6086** Civil disturbance and religious strife 1969-

.7** HISTORY OF EIRE
.7083** Southern Ireland since 1922

.8** HISTORY OF BRITISH EMPIRE

.81** HISTORY OF BRITISH COMMONWEALTH OF NATIONS

942 HISTORY OF ENGLAND

.01 Early history, 410-1066
.011 Middle Ages, 5th-15th centuries

Class here general works on the Middle Ages in England
For general works on crusades, see 940.1

.02 Normans, 1066-1154

.03 Plantagenets, 1154-1399

.04 Lancaster and York 1399-1485

.05 Tudors, 1485-1603

.06 Stuarts, 1603-1714

The following notation should be used only for material related specifically to England in the period after the Act of Union

.07 Georgian period 1714-1837
.08 Victorian era to present day
.081 Victoria, 1837-1901
.082 Edward VII, 1901-1910
.083 George V, 1910-1936
.084 Edward VIII and George VI, 1936-1952
.086 Elizabeth II, 1952-

.9 HISTORY OF WALES

.901** Early history to unification under Hywel Dda c930
.902** Wars with Normans and early Plantagenets 930-1272
.903** Invasion and conquest by Edward I

The following notation should be used only for material related specifically to Wales in the period after the conquest by Edward I in 1283

.904** Lancaster and York, 1399-1485
Owain Glyndwr's rebellion
.905** Tudors, 1485-1603
Act of Incorporation into England, 1535

942.906** Stuarts, 1603-1714
.907** Georgian period 1714-1837
.908** Victorian era to present day
.9081** Victoria, 1837-1901
.9082** Edward VII, 1901-1910
.9083** George V, 1910-1936
.9084** Edward VIII, and George VI, 1936-1952
.9086** Elizabeth II, 1952-

943 HISTORY OF CENTRAL EUROPE

For subdivisions use period notation given under 940 adding initial '0', eg., Middle Ages in Central Europe, 943.01

.1** HISTORY OF GERMANY
.103** Early history to the reformation, 486-1618
.105** 17th century and rise of Prussia, 1618-1790
.106** Napoleonic wars, 1790-1815
.107** Unification, 1815-1866
.108** Empire and Third Reich, 1866-1945
.1087** Modern Germany, 1945-

Class here materials related to Germany as a whole
For general history of Eastern Germany (German Democratic Republic), see 943.2; Western Germany (German Federal Republic), 944.1

943.2** HISTORY OF EASTERN GERMANY (GERMAN DEMOCRATIC REPUBLIC) SINCE 1945

944** HISTORY OF WESTERN EUROPE

For subdivision use period notation given under 940 adding initial '0', eg., Western Europe since 1945, 944.055

.1** HISTORY OF WESTERN GERMANY (GERMAN FEDERAL REPUBLIC) SINCE 1945

For general history of Germany, see 943.1; of East Germany, see 943.2

.4** HISTORY OF FRANCE
.402** Early history and unification, 486-1589
.404** Bourbons and the Revolution, 1589-1804
.405** First Empire, 1804-1815
.407** Early 19th century, 1815-1870
.408** Late 19th century, 20th century, 1870-

945 HISTORY OF ITALY
.01 Middle ages, 476-1453

Class here rise of city republics

.02 Renaissance to Napoleonic era, 1453-1789
.06 Napoleonic era, 1789-1814
.07** Nineteenth century to unification 1814-1870

Class here works on the Risorgimento

.08** Kingdom of Italy, 1870-1939
.082** Fascist regime and World War II, 1922-1945
.085** Modern Italy

Italy since 1945

946.1 HISTORY OF SPAIN
.103 Early history to unification, 415-1516
.105 16th and 17th centuries, 1516-1808
.106 Napoleonic era, 1808-1814
.108 19th and early 20th centuries, 1814-1939
.1082 Regime of General Franco, 1939-1975
.1083** Bourbon restoration, 1975-

947 **HISTORY OF RUSSIA AND THE USSR**

.05 Development of Russia to reign of Peter the Great, c400 to 1725

.07 18th and early 19th centuries, 1725-1855

.08 Late 19th and early 20th centuries

.084 Revolution and establishment of USSR 1916-1953

.085 Post Stalin era, 1953-

950 GENERAL HISTORY OF ASIA

For subdivision see 'Area' Table 2

960 GENERAL HISTORY OF AFRICA

For subdivision see 'Area' Table 2

970 GENERAL HISTORY OF NORTH AMERICA

.01 Discovery and exploration to c1600

.02 Colonial period, c1600 to mid 18th century

.03 Late 18th century

.04 19th century

.05 20th century

.1 North American Indians

971 HISTORY OF CANADA

.01 Discovery and exploration to 1763

.03 Early British rule and Act of Union, 1763-1840

.05 Late 19th century, Dominion of Canada, 1840-1911

.06 20th century, 1911-

973 HISTORY OF UNITED STATES

.1 Discovery and exploration to 1607

.2 Colonial period, 1607-1775

.3 Revolution and confederation, 1775-1789

.6 Early 19th century, 1789-1861

.7 Civil war, 1861-1865

.8 Late 19th century, 1865-1901

.9 20th century

980 GENERAL HISTORY OF SOUTH AMERICA

For subdivision see 'Area' Table 2

990 GENERAL HISTORY OF OTHER PARTS OF THE WORLD, OCEANIA

993 HISTORY OF NEW ZEALAND

994 HISTORY OF AUSTRALIA

.01 Discovery and exploration to 1788

.02 Colonisation, 1788-1851

.03 Colonial period, 1851-1901

.04 Early 20th century, 1901-1945

.05 Post war and Menzies administration, 1945-1965

.06 Later 20th century, 1965-

AUXILIARY TABLES

1 STANDARD SUBDIVISIONS

2 AREAS

3 LITERATURE

4 LANGUAGES

THE USE OF THE TABLES

These tables are used only in conjunction with the schedules. In some instances the numbers from one table may be added to those of another table: for this reason a summary of Table 1 is repeated in Tables 3 and 4. But in all cases numbers from one or more tables are to be used *after* the appropriate numbers from the schedules.

The dash preceding each number merely shows that the number never stands alone: it is omitted in actual use.

Each of the tables is preceded by a note indicating when it should, or may, be applied.

The use of any table is entirely optional: they are provided for use if desired.

TABLE 1: STANDARD SUBDIVISIONS

The following notations are never used alone, but *may be used if wished* with any number from the schedules: e.g., dictionaries (–03 in this table) of geography (910): 910.03; history (–09) of mathematics (510): 510.9. Note that a decimal point always follows the third digit. Note also that the 0 is not repeated – and indeed *may* be left out altogether from lengthy numbers where no confusion results with a notation already in use: see footnote to paragraph 5:3:6 of the preface.

The use of any of these standard subdivisions is entirely optional. Some of the most generally useful are included in the schedules.

–01 PHILOSOPHY AND THEORY OF THE SUBJECT

–016 Bibliographies and catalogues

–02 MISCELLANEOUS MATERIALS

–021 Statistics of the subject

–022* Illustrations and models: including charts, diagrams, material for viewing by projection

–023* Audio-visual materials: sound films, video tapes, tape–slide programmes

–024* Audio materials: tapes and records

–025 Directories relating to the subject

–028 Techniques, apparatus, operation manuals

–03 DICTIONARIES, ENCYCLOPAEDIAS of the subject

–05 PERIODICALS dealing with the subject
e.g., *Railway Magazine* 385.05

–06 ORGANISATIONS concerned with the subject

–07 STUDY AND TEACHING of the subject
including awards and prizes

–074 Museums and vivaria

–075 Collections

–09 HISTORICAL AND GEOGRAPHICAL TREATMENT

–091 Treatment by regional areas: add notation from the first page of Table 2 to base number –09: e.g., the subject in the southern hemisphere –09181

–092 Persons: biography, and critical appraisal of work, of people associated with the subject: e.g., Henry Ford 629.2092. (Consult preface, par. 5:4:1(e).)

–093–099 Treatment by specific continents, countries, or places: add 'areas' notation –3–9 from Table 2 to base number –09: e.g., the Welfare State in West Germany 360.944

Class treatment by 'natural' regions (e.g., tropics, deserts) in –091.

* For the optional use of these notations, see preface, 5:3:6(b).

TABLE 2: AREAS

The notations in this table are never used alone, but *may be used if wished* with any number from the schedules: e.g., birds (598.2) of South America (−8 in this table): 598.298; birds of forests (−152 in this table): 598.29152. The digit 9 comes from Table 1 (−09 indicating historical or geographical treatment of a topic: for omission of 0 see the footnote to paragraph 5:3:6 of the preface). Inserting this digit ensures that the new number will not conflict with any number already in the schedules.

SUMMARY

−1 Types of areas and regions

−3 The ancient world

−4−9 The modern world

−4 Europe
−5 Asia Orient Far East
−6 Africa
−7 North America
−8 South America
−9 Australasia, Oceania, Arctic and Antarctic

−11−13 ZONAL REGIONS

−11 HIGH LATITUDE ZONES
Polar regions, Tundra
−12 TEMPERATE (MID LATITUDE) ZONES
−13 TROPICAL (LOW LATITUDE) ZONE
Equatorial regions

−14−16 NATURAL ENVIRONMENTS

−14 LAND AND LAND FORMS
Mountains; plains (plateaux); valleys; particular types of soil
−141 Continental areas
−142 Islands
−146 Coastal regions (including caves)
−15 TYPES OF VEGETATION
−152 Forests
−153 Grasslands
−154 Deserts
−16 AIR AND WATER ENVIRONMENTS
−161 Atmosphere
−162 Oceans and seas
−169 Lakes and rivers
−17 SOCIAL AND ECONOMIC REGIONS
−171 Political blocs, empires
−172 Degree of economic development
e.g., 'Third World'
−173 Degree of population density Rural, suburban, urban regions
−18 OTHER KINDS OF REGIONS
−181 Hemispheres
Eastern, western; northern, southern
−182 Ocean and sea basins
e.g., Atlantic region; Pacific region
−19 SPACE

–3 THE ANCIENT WORLD

–3 ANCIENT WORLD to c 500 AD

–31 China to c 420 AD

–32 EGYPT AND NILE VALLEY to c 640 AD

–33 PALESTINE (Judea) to c 70 AD

–34 India to 647 AD

–35 MESOPOTAMIA to c 640 AD

–36 EUROPE to c 500 AD (except Mediterranean region)

–362 BRITISH ISLES to c 410 AD

–363 Germanic regions to c 500 AD

–364 Celtic regions to c 500 AD

–366 Iberian peninsula to c 500 AD

–37 ITALY and adjacent territories to 476 AD: class here the Roman Empire

–38 GREECE to 323 AD: class here Alexander's empire

–39 EASTERN MEDITERRANEAN to c 640 AD: class here the Phoenician and Carthaginian empires

Note: The ancient world is not included in the Index of Places.

–4–9 THE MODERN WORLD

–4 EUROPE

SUMMARY

–41 British Isles: Great Britain: Scotland, Ireland
–42 England and Wales
–43 Central Europe
–44 Western Europe
–45 Italy and adjacent areas
–46 Spain and Portugal
–47 Eastern Europe: U.S.S.R.
–48 Northern Europe: Scandinavia
–49 South-eastern Europe

–41 BRITISH ISLES; GREAT BRITAIN in general

–411 SCOTLAND

–411 1 Northern Scotland: Highland region and Island authorities

–412 North-eastern Scotland: Fife, Grampian, Tayside regions

–413 South-eastern Scotland: Borders, Central, Lowland regions

–413 4 Edinburgh

–414 South-western Scotland: Dumfries & Galloway, Strathclyde

–414 4 Glasgow

–415 IRELAND

–416 ULSTER, NORTHERN IRELAND

–416 1 North-east area (County of Antrim)

–416 2 Western area (Counties of Fermanagh, Londonderry, Tyrone)

–416 5 South-east area (County Down)

–416 6 Southern area (County of Armagh)

–416 7 Belfast

–416 9 Counties of Irish Republic in Ulster (Cavan, Donegal, Monaghan)

–417 EIRE, REPUBLIC OF IRELAND

–417 1 Connacht

–418 Leinster

–418 3 Dublin City

–419 Munster

–42 ENGLAND AND WALES

–421 Greater LONDON including the London Boroughs and former Middlesex

–421 2 City of London

–422 South-eastern England: Berkshire, Hampshire, Isle of Wight, Kent, Surrey, Sussex: class here works on the Home Counties, Thames valley

–423 South-western England. Avon, Cornwall, Devon, Dorset, Somerset, Wiltshire, Scilly Is., Channel Is.

–424 Midlands: Gloucestershire, Hereford & Worcester, Salop, Staffordshire, Warwickshire, West Midlands met. County

–424 96 Birmingham

–425 East Midlands: Bedford, Buckinghamshire, Derbyshire, Hertfordshire, Leicestershire, Lincolnshire, Northamptonshire, Nottinghamshire, Oxfordshire: class here works on Peak District, Trent valley

–426 Eastern England, East Anglia: Cambridgeshire (with Hunts.), Essex, Norfolk Suffolk: general works on the Fens

–427 North-western England: Cheshire, Cumbria, Lancashire; Isle of Man; met. counties of Greater Manchester, Merseyside

–427 33 Manchester

–427 53 Liverpool

−428 North-eastern England: Cleveland, Durham, Humberside, Tyne & Wear, Northumberland, Yorkshire (all parts): class here general works on Pennines

−428 19 Leeds

−428 21 Sheffield

−429 WALES

−429 1 North Wales: Clwyd, Gwynedd

−429 4 South Wales: Dyfed, Glamorgan, Gwent, Powys

−429 8 Cardiff

−43 CENTRAL EUROPE

−431** GERMANY (as a whole)

−432** EAST GERMANY (D.D.R.) (for West Germany see −441)

−436 AUSTRIA, Liechtenstein

−437 CZECHOSLOVAKIA

−438 POLAND

−439 HUNGARY

−44 WESTERN EUROPE

−441** WEST GERMANY (German Federal Republic): class works on Germany as a whole in −431

−442** BELGIUM, Luxembourg

−443** NETHERLANDS

−444** FRANCE

−447** SWITZERLAND; The Alps

−45 ITALY including Sicily, Corsica, Sardinia, Malta

−46 IBERIAN PENINSULA

−461 SPAIN (Andorra, Balearic Is.: for Canary Is. see −64)

−468 GIBRALTAR

−469 PORTUGAL including Azores, Madeira

−47 EASTERN EUROPE, U.S.S.R. (For Asiatic Russia see −57)

−48 NORTHERN EUROPE, SCANDINAVIA

−481 NORWAY

−482 SWEDEN

−487** FINLAND

−489 DENMARK including Faroe Islands, Iceland

−49 SOUTH-EASTERN EUROPE

−495 GREECE

−496 BALKAN PENINSULA including Albania

−497 BULGARIA, YUGOSLAVIA

−498 RUMANIA

−499 AEGEAN SEA ISLANDS; including CRETE

−5 ASIA; THE FAR EAST
Class here general works on Eurasia

−51 CHINA including Outer Mongolia; Taiwan (Formosa)

−512 HONG KONG

−515 Tibet

−519 Korea

−52 JAPAN and adjacent islands

−53 ARABIAN PENINSULA including Persian Gulf and Sinai Peninsula

−54 INDIA including Himalayan states

−549 PAKISTAN

−549 1 BANGLADESH

−549 3 SRI LANKA (Ceylon)

−55 IRAN (Persia)

−56 MIDDLE EAST

−561 TURKEY including Turkey in Europe, Istanbul

−564 Cyprus

−567 Iraq

−569 Eastern Mediterranean

−569 1 Syria

−569 2 Lebanon

−569 4 ISRAEL (Palestine)

−569 5 Jordan

−57 SIBERIA (ASIATIC RUSSIA)

−58 CENTRAL ASIA including Afghanistan, Baluchistan, Soviet Republics of Central Asia, Transcaucasia

−59 SOUTH-EAST ASIA

−591 Burma

−593 Thailand (Siam)

−594 Laos

−595 Malaysia, Singapore, Brunei

−596 Khmer Republic (Cambodia)

−597 Vietnam

−598 Indonesia

−599 Philippine Islands

−6 AFRICA

−61 LIBYA, TUNISIA

−62 EGYPT, SUDAN, SUEZ (for Sinai see −53)

−63 ETHIOPIA (Abyssinia)

−64 NORTH-WEST AFRICA including offshore islands

−65 ALGERIA

–66 WEST AFRICA: class here general works on the Sahara

–667 Ghana

–669 Nigeria

–67 CENTRAL & EAST AFRICA

–675 Zaire (Congo Rep.)

–676 Uganda, Kenya

–678 Tanzania

–679 Mozambique

–68 SOUTHERN AFRICA

–689 Malawi, Rhodesia (Zimbabwe), Zambia

–69 Malagasy (Madagascar), Mauritius, Reunion Is., Seychelles Is.

–7 NORTH AMERICA
Class here works dealing with both American continents

–701 North American Indians

–71 CANADA (for Alaska see –73)

–711 British Columbia

–712 Northern Territories and Prairie Provinces

–713 Ontario

–714 Quebec

–715 Eastern Provinces

–718 Newfoundland, Labrador

–72 MEXICO & CENTRAL AMERICAN STATES (for Panama see –86)

–728 Central America

–729 West Indies Islands including Bermuda, Leeward & Windward Is.

–73 UNITED STATES

–74 North-eastern states

–75 South-eastern (Atlantic seaboard) states

–76 Gulf coast states and south central states

–77 Lake states and north central states

–78 Western (mountain and plain) states

–79 Pacific coast states; Alaska

–8 SOUTH AMERICA
Class here general works on Latin America, Spanish America, the Andes

–801 South American Indians

–81 Brazil

–82 Argentine Rep., Patagonia

–83 Chile

–84 Bolivia

–85 Peru

–86 Colombia, Ecuador, Panama

–87 Venezuela

–88 Guyana

–89 Paraguay, Uruguay

–9 OCEANIA AND POLAR REGIONS
Class here comprehensive works on the islands of the world

–93 NEW ZEALAND and MELANESIA

–94 AUSTRALIA

–941 Western Australia

–942 Central Australia (South Australia & Northern Territories)

–943 Queensland

–944 New South Wales

–945 Victoria

–946 Tasmania

–947 Australian Capital Territory (Canberra)

–95 NEW GUINEA

–96 POLYNESIA: Central and South Pacific islands

–969 Hawaii

–97 Islands of the Atlantic Ocean, including Falkland Is., St Helena, Ascension, Tristan da Cunha

–98 ARCTIC ISLANDS AND ANTARCTICA: including Greenland, North Pole, South Pole

TABLE 3: LITERATURE

SUBDIVISIONS OF INDIVIDUAL LITERATURES

The three sets of notations in this table are never used alone, but may be added, as required, to the base number for an individual literature (marked with * in the schedules). A decimal point always stands between the third and fourth digits. Standard subdivisions or period subdivisions are added *after* the specific form divisions (if used: for alternatives see preface 5:4:1(b)). E.g. English (base number 82) poetry 821; anthologies of English poetry 821.08; Victorian poetry 821.8 (if the period notation is adopted). Greek (base number 88) drama 882; history (and appraisal) of Greek drama 882.09.

–01–09 STANDARD SUBDIVISIONS

–01 Philosophy and theory
–016 Bibliographies and catalogues
–022* Visual treatment of the subject: illustrations, slides etc.
–023* Audio-visual materials
–024* Audio materials: tapes, records
–03 Dictionaries, encyclopaedias, concordances
–05 Periodicals
–06 Organisations
–07 Study and teaching; prizes
–08 Collections; anthologies containing works of several authors
–09 History of the subject (including critical studies)

–1–8 SPECIFIC FORM DIVISIONS

Class description, critical appraisal, and collected works of an individual author with the form with which he is chiefly identified. (But for alternatives to using the specific form divisions see preface 5:4:1(b). If any of the alternatives is adopted, some details in the notes to this table will need adjustment.)

–1 Poetry
–2 Drama
–3 Fiction
–4 Essays
–7 Satire and humour
–8 Miscellaneous works:

Collected works of an individual author writing in a variety of forms
For an optional alternative use of –8 see preface 5:4:1(b)

Any of these form divisions may be subdivided by using standard subdivisions: e.g.,
anthologies of English poetry 821.08
history of French drama 842.09
indexes of English fiction 823.03
English satirical periodicals 827.05

---

* For the optional use of these notations see preface 5:3:6(b).

–1–914 PERIOD SUBDIVISIONS FOR ENGLISH LITERATURE

–1	Early English	1066–1400
–2	Pre-Elizabethan	1400–1558
–3	Elizabethan	1558–1625
–33	Shakespeare	
–4	17th century	1625–1702
–5	Early 18th century	1702–1745
–6	Later 18th century	1745–1800
–7	Early 19th century	1800–1837
–8	Victorian	1837–1900
–9	Post-Victorian	1900–
–91	20th century	
–912	Early 20th century	1900–1945
–914	Later 20th century	1945–

TABLE 4: LANGUAGES

SUBDIVISIONS OF INDIVIDUAL LANGUAGES

The notations in this table are never used alone, but may be added, as required, to the base number for an individual language (marked with * in the schedules). A decimal point always stands between the third and fourth digits. Standard subdivisions are added *after* the language form divisions: e.g., dictionaries of English slang 427.03; teaching of French grammar 445.07.

–01–07 STANDARD SUBDIVISIONS

–01 Philosophy and theory
–016 Bibliographies and catalogues
–022* Visual treatment of the subject
–023* Audio-visual materials
–024* Audio materials: tapes, records
–03 Encyclopaedias, concordances
Class *dictionaries* of the standard form of the language in 'Language Form' division 3
–05 Periodicals
–06 Organisations
–07 Study and teaching of language

–1–8 LANGUAGE FORM DIVISIONS

–1 Standard form of the language (written and spoken)
Including abbreviations, acronyms, alphabets, pronunciation, punctuation, spelling

–2 Etymology, derivations
Phonetic development including foreign elements

–3 Dictionaries
Including bilingual dictionaries; dictionaries of abbreviations, synonyms etc.

Class a bilingual dictionary with the language with which it will be more useful: e.g., a German–English dictionary will probably be classified with German (433) in an English library

5 Grammar: structural system

–7 Non-standard forms of the language
Dialects; regional and earlier variations; slang

–8 Practical works: textbooks for learning the language
Class here the language for foreigners

INDEX

THE USE OF THE INDEX

The index consists of two parts, an index of places and a relative index of subjects.

The index of places. This provides notations for both history and geography. (Where local studies of places or areas in the British Isles are concerned, some librarians may find it simpler to ignore the geography notation and use only that for history, as the line is often difficult to draw.) The index of places relates closely to Table 2 (Areas and to the endpaper maps, where much of the same information is presented in a different form.

Alphabetical order. Both the index of places and the subject index are arranged in a word-by-word sequence (a method made familiar by its use in telephone directories). Thus all entries which include the word 'new' plus another word will precede those in which 'new' is part of a longer word:

New England	NOT	New England	New Testament	NOT	Newspapers
New Guinea		Newfoundland	New Year		New Testament
New Hebrides		New Guinea	Newspapers		Newts
New Zealand		New Hebrides	Newts		New Year
Newfoundland		New Zealand			

In acronyms (e.g., U.N.E.S.C.O.) each letter is treated as a word in applying the above rule. The effect generally is to bring all acronyms to the beginning of the sequence for any letter.

The subject index (relative index). The Dewey classification schedules represent one sequential arrangement of man's knowledge of himself and of his physical and social environment. As modern man extends that knowledge the number of possible and valid arrangements constantly increases, the boundaries between subjects become increasingly indistinct, the interrelations ever more complex. And yet it is often these interrelations that are the theme of modern publications.

The aim of this index, therefore, is not only to provide a guide to the subjects named in the schedules and tables but also to indicate their relationships and links with other subjects. Thus in addition to entries for major subjects, such as science, art, physics, photography etc., there are entries for topics which embrace more than one subject. The entry for water is an example. Scientifically, water may be studied as an aspect of physics or chemistry, yet its presence or absence affects many other aspects of man's life and his environment. Man needs a water supply not only for his own biological functions but also for the agriculture which supplies his food and the raw materials for industry; the physical and chemical behaviour of water with changes of temperature and pressure is the basis of meteorology and also of geological processes; man uses water as a means of transport, organises sports on it or in it, harnesses the power of falling water to further his industrial activities, which often cause pollution of rivers and lakes. The entry for water therefore includes references to a wide range of subjects. It is for this reason that the index is referred to as a 'relative index' – relating, as it does, one aspect of a subject to another.

The relationship of the various aspects is shown by the indentation of the entry. For example, handwriting is not simply a matter of calligraphy; it can also be analysed, either for crime detection or for personality analysis. The entry reflects this relationship thus:

Handwriting	
analysis	
crime detection	351.74
popular psychology	133.3
calligraphy	745.6

Synonyms. Many synonyms are given. For instance 'locomotives' will be found as well as 'engines'. But obviously not every synonym can be included without making the index over-long. So it may be necessary to look for an alternative name (e.g., for 'cloth' see 'textile'), or to look under a broader subject name (e.g., for 'apples' see 'fruit').

Using the index. Opposite each entry is given its notation or classification number. (That on the left is the one recommended for primary schools: see preface, paragraph 4:2:3.) Since these numbers determine the order of items on the shelves and cards in the classified catalogue, the subject index is a guide to both. It should therefore be the first point the user comes to in his search.

The index is a guide to the schedules, not a substitute for them. Its use in classification should be to guide the classifier to the most likely notation for the subject of the item. The schedules themselves should then be carefully examined before deciding on a class number. For example checking the index for a class number for a book on the gods of ancient Greece and Rome will reveal 290 Mythology; but checking with the schedules will reveal a more specific notation 292 for Roman and Greek mythology. Alternatively, since the object of classification is to place an item where it will be seen by the greatest number of potential users, the index may be used to check that a possible relationship with another subject has not been overlooked, and to suggest useful added entries for the catalogue.

The school's own subject index. The two indexes in this book cannot as they stand provide an index to a particular school collection, for four main reasons::

(a) No school collection will encompass every subject named in the schedules. In compiling a subject index for his own collection, therefore, the school librarian will need to select those entries which refer to the subjects actually covered by his stock.

(b) Some of the entries given, whilst sufficient to guide the classifier, will not be specific enough. A child seeking information on Roman mythology will find the entry 'Gods and goddesses: mythology 290' too vague. The school librarian needs to expand his own index to include an entry 'Roman gods 292.937'.

(c) The school librarian can make additional entries in his own subject index showing simpler or more familiar terms used in the school but not appearing in the printed index. For instance an entry may be added for picture writing as well as hieroglyphics. Names of animals, plants or people may be added if likely to be looked for often by pupils.

(d) The arrangement of the Index of places might be too complex for younger children who would, therefore, need specific entries for the geography and history of each country in the school's subject index, e.g.

British Isles	
geography	914.1
history	
ancient	936.2
modern	941

It has been customary to make the school's subject index on cards, with all indented entries given under the main topic included, e.g.

LAMPS	
electrical engineering	621.3
household equipment	643
lighting systems	621.32
street lighting	628.9

This has the advantage that, as items on new subjects are acquired or subject names not already included come to light, cards for additional entries can be written and inserted easily. It has the disadvantage that pupils who do not know their alphabet thoroughly may find the filing sequence confusing. Also long entries (e.g., water) may over-run and need two or even three cards. Lists in sheet or book form enable the reader to scan a number of entries at a glance. Unfortunately, when additional entries are later needed, one has to recast the whole page. It is possible, however, to retain the advantages of both methods if a strip index is used, each line being typed or written on a separable strip to be inserted into a frame. Thus for example the following entries might have been needed initially:

WATER	
chemistry	546
conservation	333.9
ecology	
freshwater	574.929
irrigation	631.7
physics	532
pollution	
public health	363.4
water supply	628.1
power	621.2
sports	797

If at a later date materials on marine ecology, hydro-electric generation, and water polo are acquired, a strip (correctly indented) would be prepared for each, and inserted in place:

WATER	
chemistry	546
conservation	333.9
ecology	
freshwater	574.929
marine (sea)	574.921
irrigation	631.7
physics	532
pollution	
public health	363.4
water supply	628.1
polo	797.2
power	621.2
hydro-electric	621.31
sports	797

In this way one can create a useful working index which can be easily consulted by all library users, including the child who is uncertain of alphabetical order.

Revising the index. Section 5:4:3 of the preface, referring to the expansion or reduction of the schedules to meet individual school requirements, ends by stressing the need to examine *every* index entry that might be affected. Where the schedules are modified the index as it stands would become misleading. (If however the school's own subject index is compiled as suggested above, this revision is done automatically.)

Ensuring that all index entries are revised is a difficult and time-consuming task. Accuracy depends on examining simultaneously all entries for a given notation. For this reason the compiler of this *Introduction* has also compiled a version of the subject index organised in a classified sequence: this may be purchased separately.*

Alternatively the teacher-librarian may compile his own classified index. He could use 6″ x 4″ catalogue cards and head them with the notations from the schedules, thus:

513	621.38	651

It is then possible – though very time-consuming – to go through the index and list on the cards all subject entries relating to the notation. Where entries are indented it is necessary to include all words of the entry, thus:

513	621.38	651
Adding machines mathematics	Adding machines manufacture	Adding machines office equipment

When the schedules are expanded or contracted (and similarly when options are adopted) the appropriate notations can be examined in the classified index and all the affected entries can be quickly and accurately amended.

---

* Enquiries addressed to Mr B. A. J. Winslade, c/o The School Library Association, will be forwarded.

INDEX OF PLACES

This index is a guide to the 'Areas' notation given in Table 2, which is added to the base number 91 to give a number for geography, description and travel, and to the base number 9 to give a number for history: see the notes in the schedules (at 914–919 and 930–990). Lower case type is used for places in the United Kingdom, capitals for the rest of the world. Names in italics are the former (and probably better known) names of countries whose names were changed. For the ancient world see the subject index.

914.294	Brecon (former county)	942.94
917.11	BRITISH COLUMBIA	971.1
917.2	BRITISH HONDURAS	972
914.1	British Isles	941
915.95	BRUNEI	959.5
914.25	Buckinghamshire	942.5
914.97	BULGARIA	949.7
915.91	BURMA	959.1
916.7	BURUNDI (*RUANDA–URUNDI*)	967
914.14	Bute (former county)	941.4

C

914.291	Caernarvon (former county)	942.91
914.111	Caithness (former county)	941.11
915.96	*CAMBODIA* (KHMER REPUBLIC)	959.6
914.26	Cambridgeshire	942.6
916.7	CAMEROUN – UNITED REPUBLIC	967
916.7	CAMEROUNS	967
917.1	CANADA	971
917.11	BRITISH COLUMBIA	971.1
917.15	EASTERN PROVINCES	971.5
917.18	LABRADOR	971.8
917.11	MOUNTAIN PROVINCES	971.1
917.18	NEWFOUNDLAND	971.8
917.12	NORTHERN TERRITORIES	971.2
917.13	ONTARIO	971.3
917.12	PRAIRIE PROVINCES	971.2
917.14	QUEBEC	971.4
916.4	CANARY ISLANDS	964
919.47	CANBERRA – AUSTRALIA	994.7
916.6	CAPE VERDE ISLANDS	966
914.298	Cardiff	942.98
914.294	Cardigan (former county)	942.94
917.29	CARIBBEAN ISLANDS	972.9
914.294	Carmarthen (former county)	942.94
914.169	CAVAN COUNTY – EIRE	941.69
915.98	*CELEBES IS* (SULAWESI)	959.8
916.7	CENTRAL AFRICA	967
916.7	CENTRAL AFRICAN REPUBLIC (*UBANGI–SHARI*)	967
917.2	CENTRAL AMERICA	972
915.8	CENTRAL ASIA	958
914.3	CENTRAL EUROPE	943
919.6	CENTRAL PACIFIC ISLANDS	996
914.13	Central Region – Scotland	941.3
915.493	*CEYLON* (SRI LANKA)	954.93
916.7	CHAD REPUBLIC	967
914.23	Channel Islands	942.3
914.27	Cheshire	942.7
918.3	CHILE	983
915.1	CHINA	951
919.6	CHRISTMAS ISLANDS	996
914.13	Clackmannan (former county)	941.3
914.28	Cleveland	942.8
914.291	Clwyd – Wales	942.91
918.6	COLOMBIA	986
	Commonwealth, British	941.81
916.7	CONGO	967
916.7	CONGOLESE PEOPLE'S REPUBLIC	967
914.171	CONNACHT – EIRE	941.71
919.6	COOK ISLANDS	996
914.23	Cornwall	942.3
914.5	CORSICA	945
917.2	COSTA RICA	972
914.99	CRETE	949.9
917.29	CUBA	972.9
914.27	Cumberland (former county)	942.7
914.27	Cumbria	942.7
915.6	CYPRUS	956
914.37	CZECHOSLOVAKIA	943.7

D

914.23	Dartmoor	942.3
916.6	DAHOMEY	966
914.96	DANUBE	949.6
914.291	Denbigh (former county)	942.91
914.89	DENMARK	948.9
914.25	Derbyshire	942.5
914.23	Devon	942.3
917.29	DOMINICAN REPUBLIC	972.9
914.169	DONEGAL COUNTY – EIRE	941.69
914.23	Dorset	942.3
914.165	Down (former county)	941.65
914.22	Downs – general works	942.2
914.183	DUBLIN	941.83
914.14	Dumbarton (fomer county)	941.4
914.14	Dumfries and Galloway Region – Scotland	941.4
914.28	Durham	942.8
918.8	*DUTCH GUIANA* (SURINAM)	988
914.294	Dyfed – Wales	942.94

E

915	EAST, THE	950
916.7	EAST AFRICA	967
914.26	East Anglia	942.6
914.32	EAST GERMANY	943.2
915.98	EAST INDIES	959.8
914.13	East Lothian (former county)	941.3
914.25	East Midlands – England	942.5
915.491	*EAST PAKISTAN* (BANGLADESH)	954.91
914.22	East Sussex	942.2
919.6	EASTER ISLANDS	996
915	EASTERN ASIA	950
914.26	Eastern England	942.6
914.7	EASTERN EUROPE	947
910.9181	EASTERN HEMISPHERE	909.9181
914.111	Eastern Highlands – Scotland	941.11

915	EASTERN WORLD	950
918.6	ECUADOR	986
914.134	Edinburgh	941.34
916.2	EGYPT	962
914.17	EIRE	941.7
917.2	EL SALVADOR	972
914.2	England	942
916.7	EQUATORIAL GUINEA, REPUBLIC OF (*SPANISH GUINEA*)	
914.26	Essex	942.6
914.47	ESTONIA	947
916.3	ETHIOPIA (*ABYSSINIA*)	963
915	EURASIA	950
914	EUROPE	940
914.3	CENTRAL	943
914.7	EASTERN	947
914.8	NORTHERN	948
914.9	SOUTH EASTERN	949
914.4	WESTERN	944
914.7	EUROPEAN RUSSIA	947
914.23	Exmoor	942.3

F

915	FAR EAST	950
914.89	Faroe Islands	948.9
914.41	FEDERAL REPUBLIC OF GERMANY	944.1
914.26	Fenland	942.6
914.162	Fermanagh (former county)	941.62
914.12	Fife Region – Scotland	941.2
914.12	Fife (former county)	941.2
919.6	FIJI ISLANDS	996
914.87	FINLAND	948.7
914.291	Flint (former county)	942.91
915.1	*FORMOSA* (TAIWAN)	951
914.44	FRANCE	944.4
918.8	FRENCH GUIANA (*GUYANE*)	988

G

916.7	GABON	967
914.14	Galloway (former county)	941.4
916.6	GAMBIA	966
915.3	GAZA STRIP	953
914.32	GERMAN DEMOCRATIC REPUBLIC	943.2
914.41	GERMAN FEDERAL REPUBLIC	944.1
	GERMANY	
914.31	COMPREHENSIVE WORKS	943.1
914.32	EAST	943.2
914.41	WEST	944.1
916.67	GHANA	966.7
914.68	GIBRALTAR	946.8
919.6	GILBERT AND ELLICE ISLANDS	996
914.294	Glamorgan	942.94
914.144	Glasgow	941.44
914.24	Gloucestershire	942.4
915.1	GOBI DESERT	951
914.12	Grampian Region – Scotland	941.2
914.1	Great Britain	941
914.21	Greater London	942.1
914.27	Greater Manchester, Metropolitan County of	942.7
914.95	GREECE	949.5
919.8	GREENLAND	998
917.2	GUATEMALA	972
914.23	Guernsey	942.3
918.8	GUIANAS	988
916.6	GUINEA (*FRENCH GUINEA*)	966
916.6	GUINEA, PORTUGUESE	966
918.8	GUYANA (*BRITISH GUIANA*)	986
918.8	*GUYANE* (FRENCH GUIANA)	988
914.294	Gwent – Wales	942.94
914.291	Gwynedd – Wales	942.91

H

914.28	Hadrian's Wall – general works	936.2
917.29	HAITI	972.9
914.22	Hampshire	942.2
919.69	HAWAII	996.9
	Hebrides	
914.111	Inner; Outer	941.11
919.3	NEW	993
914.24	Hereford and Worcester	942.4
914.24	Hereford (former county)	942.4
914.25	Hertfordshire	942.5
914.111	Highland Region – Scotland	941.11
915.4	HIMALAYAS	954
914.43	HOLLAND	944.3
914.22	Home Counties	942.2
917.2	HONDURAS	972
915.12	HONGKONG	951.2
914.28	Humberside	942.8
914.39	HUNGARY	943.9
914.26	Huntingdon (former county)	942.6

I

914.6	IBERIAN PENINSULA	946
914.89	ICELAND	948.9
915.4	INDIA	954
916.9	INDIAN OCEAN ISLANDS	969
915.98	INDIES, EAST	959.8
917.29	INDIES, WEST	972.9
915.9	INDO-CHINA	959
915.98	INDONESIA	959.8
914.111	Inner Hebrides	941.11
914.111	Inverness (former county)	941.11
915.5	IRAN (*PERSIA*)	955
915.67	IRAQ	956.7
	Ireland	
914.15	General: whole island	941.5
914.16	Northern	941.6
914.17	REPUBLIC OF	941.7
914.17	IRISH FREE STATE	941.7
914.111	Islands Region – Scotland	941.11
914.27	Isle of Man	942.7

914.22	Isle of Wight	942.2
915.694	ISRAEL (*PALESTINE*)	956.94
914.5	ITALY	945
916.6	IVORY COAST	966
	J	
917.29	JAMAICA	972.9
915.2	JAPAN	952
915.98	JAVA	959.8
914.23	Jersey	942.3
915.695	JORDAN	956.95
914.97	JUGOSLAVIA	949.7
	K	
915.98	KALIMANTAN (*BORNEO*)	959.8
914.22	Kent	942.2
916.76	KENYA	967.6
915.96	KHMER REPUBLIC (*CAMBODIA*)	959.6
914.12	Kincardine (former county)	941.2
914.12	Kinross (former county)	941.2
914.14	Kirkcudbright (former county)	941.4
915.19	KOREA	951.9
915.3	KUWAIT	953
	L	
917.18	LABRADOR	971.8
914.27	Lake District	942.7
914.14	Lanark (former county)	941.4
914.27	Lancashire	942.7
915.94	LAOS	959.4
914.8	LAPLAND	948
918	LATIN AMERICA	980
914.7	LATVIA	947
915.692	LEBANON	956.92
914.2819	Leeds	942.819
917.29	LEEWARD ISLANDS	972.9
914.254	Leicestershire	942.54
914.18	LEINSTER – EIRE	941.8
916.8	LESOTHO (*BASUTOLAND*)	968
915.69	LEVANT	956.9
916.6	LIBERIA	966
916.1	LIBYA	961
914.36	LIECHTENSTEIN	943.6
914.25	Lincolnshire	942.5
914.7	LITHUANIA	947
914.2753	Liverpool	942.753
	London	
914.21	Boroughs	942.1
914.212	City of	942.12
914.212	General works	942.12
914.21	Greater	942.1
914.162	Londonderry (former county)	941.62
914.13	Lothian Region – Scotland	941.3
914.42/3	LOW COUNTRIES	944.2/3
914.42	LUXEMBOURG	944.2
	M	
915.1	MACAO	951
916.9	MADAGASCAR (*MALAGASY REPUBLIC*)	969
914.69	MADEIRA ISLANDS	946.9
916.9	*MALAGASY REPUBLIC* (MADAGASCAR)	969
916.89	MALAWI (*NYASALAND*)	968.9
915.9	MALAY ARCHIPELAGO	959
915.95	MALAYA	959.5
915.95	MALAYSIA	959.5
915.4	MALDIVE ISLANDS	954
916.6	MALI	966
914.5	MALTA	945
915.98	MALUKU (*MOLUCCA IS*)	959.8
914.27	Man, Isle of	942.7
	Manchester	
914.2733	City of	942.733
914.27	Metropolitan County	942.7
919.6	MARIANA ISLANDS	996
916.6	MAURITANIA	966
916.9	MAURITIUS	969
919.3	MELANESIA	993
914.291	Merioneth (former county)	942.91
914.27	Merseyside, Metropolitan County of	942.7
	Metropolitan County of	
914.27	Greater Manchester	942.7
914.27	Merseyside	942.7
914.28	South Yorkshire	942.8
914.28	Tyne and Wear	942.8
914.24	West Midlands	942.4
914.28	West Yorkshire	942.8
917.2	MEXICO	972
914.294	Mid Glamorgan	942.94
915.6	MIDDLE EAST	956
914.21	Middlesex (former county)	942.1
	Midlands of England	
914.25	East	942.5
914.24	General	942.4
914.24	West	942.4
914.13	Midlothian (former county)	941.3
915.98	*MOLUCCA IS* (MALUKU)	959.8
914.44	MONACO	944.4
914.169	MONAGHAN COUNTY – EIRE	941.69
915.1	MONGOLIA	951
915.1	MONGOLIAN PEOPLE'S REPUBLIC	951
914.294	Monmouth (former county)	942.94
914.294	Montgomery (former county)	942.94
914.12	Moray (former county)	941.2
916.4	MOROCCO	964
916.79	MOZAMBIQUE	967.9
914.19	MUNSTER – EIRE	941.9
915.3	MUSCAT AND OMAN	953
	N	
914.111	Nairn (former county)	941.11
916.8	NAMIBIA (*S W AFRICA*)	968
916.8	NATAL	968
915.6	NEAR EAST	956

915.4 NEPAL 954
914.43 NETHERLANDS 944.3
919.3 NEW CALEDONIA 993
917.4 NEW ENGLAND – U S A 974
919.5 NEW GUINEA 995
919.3 NEW HEBRIDES 993
919.44 NEW SOUTH WALES – AUSTRALIA 994.4
919.3 NEW ZEALAND 993
917.18 NEWFOUNDLAND 971.8
917.2 NICARAGUA 972
916.6 NIGER 966
916.69 NIGERIA 966.9
916.2 NILE VALLEY 962
914.26 Norfolk 942.6
916.1 NORTH AFRICA 961
917 NORTH AMERICA 970
915.95 NORTH BORNEO 959.5
914.22 North Downs 942.2
919.8 NORTH POLE 998
914.291 North Wales 942.91
914.28 North Yorkshire 942.8
914.25 Northamptonshire 942.5
914.28 Northeastern England 942.8
914.8 NORTHERN EUROPE 948
910.9181 NORTHERN HEMI-SPHERE 909.9181
914.6 NORTHERN IRELAND 941.6
916.89 *NORTHERN RHODESIA* (ZAMBIA) 958.9
NORTHERN TERRITORY
919.42 AUSTRALIA 994.2
917.12 CANADA 971.2
914.28 Northumberland 942.8
916.4 NORTHWEST AFRICA 964
914.27 Northwestern England 942.7
914.81 NORWAY 948.1
914.25 Nottinghamshire 942.5
915.98 NUSA TENGGARA (*LESSER SUNDA IS*) 959.8
916.89 *NYASALAND* (MALAWI) 968.9

O

919 OCEANIA 990
915.3 OMAN 953
917.3 ONTARIO 971.3
915 ORIENT 950
914.111 Orkney Islands 941.11
914.111 Outer Hebrides 941.11
915.1 OUTER MONGOLIA 951
914.25 Oxfordshire 942.5

P

911.82 PACIFIC OCEAN 901.82
919.3 ISLANDS 993
915.49 PAKISTAN 954.9
915.694 *PALESTINE* (ISRAEL) 956.94
918.6 PANAMA 986
918.6 PANAMA CANAL ZONE 986
919.5 PAPUA 995
918.9 PARAGUAY 989
914.25 Peak District 942.5
914.13 Peebles (former county) 941.3
914.294 Pembroke (former county) 942.94
914.28 Pennines – general works 942.8
915.5 *PERSIA* (IRAN) 955
915.3 PERSIAN GULF 953
914.12 Perthshire (former county) 941.2
918.5 PERU 985
914.26 Peterborough, Soke of (former county) 942.6
915.99 PHILIPPINES 959.9
919.6 PITCAIRN ISLANDS 996
914.38 POLAND 943.8
919.6 POLYNESIA 996
914.69 PORTUGAL 946.9
916.6 PORTUGUESE GUINEA 966
914.24 Potteries 942.4
914.294 Powys – Wales 942.94
914.31 PRUSSIA 943.1
917.29 PUERTO RICO 972.9

Q

915.3 QATAR 953
917.14 QUEBEC 971.4
919.43 QUEENSLAND 994.3

R

914.294 Radnor (former county) 942.94
915.3 RED SEA 953
914.14 Renfrew (former county) 941.4
916.7 REPUBLIC OF EQUATORIAL GUINEA (*SPANISH GUINEA*) 967
914.17 REPUBLIC OF IRELAND 941.7
916.9 RÉUNION 969
916.89 RHODESIA (*SOUTHERN RHODESIA*) 968.9
914.5 ROME 945
914.111 Ross and Cromarty (former county) 941.11
914.13 Roxburgh (former county) 941.3
916.7 *RUANDA-URUNDI* (RWANDA, BURUNDI) 967
914.98 RUMANIA 949.8
915.7 RUSSIA, ASIATIC 957
914.7 RUSSIA, EUROPEAN 947
914.25 Rutland (former county) 942.5
916.7 RWANDA (*RUANDA-URUNDI*) 967

S

915.95 SABAH (*NORTH BORNEO*) 959.5
916.6 SAHARA DESERT 966
919.7 ST HELENA ISLAND 997
914.23 Salisbury Plain 942.3
914.24 Salop 942.4
919.6 SAMOA 996
914.5 SAN MARINO 945
916.6 SAO TOMÉ E PRINCIPE 966
915.95 SARAWAK 959.5
914.5 SARDINIA 945
915.3 SAUDI ARABIA 953
914.8 SCANDINAVIA 948
914.23 Scilly Isles 942.3
914.11 Scotland 941.1
914.111 Scottish Highlands 941.11

916.6 SENEGAL 966
914.13 Selkirk (former county) 941.3
914.24 Severn River 942.4
916.9 SEYCHELLES 969
914.2821 Sheffield 942.821
914.111 Shetland Isles 941.11
914.24 Shropshire (former county) 942.4
915.93 *SIAM* (THAILAND) 959.3
915.7 SIBERIA 957
914.5 SICILY 945
916.6 SIERRA LEONE 966
915.4 SIKKIM 954
915.3 SINAI PENINSULA 953
915.95 SINGAPORE 959.5
914.291 Snowdonia 942.91
919.3 SOLOMON ISLANDS 993
916.7 SOMALIA 967
914.23 Somerset 942.3
916.8 SOUTH AFRICA, REPUBLIC OF 968
916.8 SOUTH AFRICA – REGION 968
918 SOUTH AMERICA 980
919.42 SOUTH AUSTRALIA 994.2
914.22 South Downs 942.2
914.294 South Glamorgan 942.94
919.6 SOUTH PACIFIC ISLANDS 996
919.8 SOUTH POLE 998
914.294 South Wales 942.94
914.28 South Yorkshire, Metropolitan County of 942.8
915.9 SOUTHEAST ASIA 959
914.22 Southeastern England 942.2
914.9 SOUTHEASTERN EUROPE 949
910.9181 SOUTHERN HEMISPHERE 909.9181
916.89 *SOUTHERN RHODESIA* (RHODESIA) 968.9
916.8 *SOUTHWEST AFRICA* (NAMIBIA) 968
914.23 Southwestern England 942.3
915.8 SOVIET REPUBLICS OF CENTRAL ASIA 958
914.7 SOVIET UNION 947
914.61 SPAIN 946.1
918 SPANISH AMERICA 980
916.7 *SPANISH GUINEA*, (REPUBLIC OF EQUATORIAL GUINEA) 967
916.4 SPANISH SAHARA 964
915.493 SRI LANKA (*CEYLON*) 954.93
914.24 Staffordshire 942.4
914.141 Strathclyde Region 941.41
914.13 Stirling (former county) 941.3
916.2 SUDAN 962
916.2 SUEZ 962
914.26 Suffolk 942.6
915.98 SULAWESI (*CELEBES IS*) 959.8
915.98 SUMATRA 959.8
915.98 SUNDA ISLANDS 959.8
918.8 SURINAM 988
914.22 Surrey 942.2
914.22 Sussex 942.2
914.111 Sutherland (former county) 941.11
916.8 SWAZILAND 968
914.85 SWEDEN 948.5
914.47 SWITZERLAND 944.7
915.691 SYRIA 956.91

T

919.6 TAHITI 996
915.1 TAIWAN (*FORMOSA*) 951
916.78 *TANGANYIKA* (TANZANIA) 967.8
916.78 TANZANIA (*TANGANYIKA*) 967.8
919.46 TASMANIA 994.6
914.12 Tayside Region – Scotland 941.2
914.22 Thames River 942.2
915.93 THAILAND (*SIAM*) 959.3
915.15 TIBET 951.5
915.98 TIMOR 959.8
916.6 TOGO 966
919.6 TONGA 996
915.8 TRANSCAUCASIA 958
914.25 Trent River 942.5
919.7 TRISTAN DA CUNHA 997
916.1 TUNISIA 961
915.61 TURKEY 956.1
914.28 Tyne and Wear, Metropolitan County of 942.8
914.36 TYROL 943.6
914.162 Tyrone (former county) 941.62

U

914.1 U K 941
917.3 U S A 973
914.7 U S S R 947
916.7 *UBANGI-SHARI* (CENTRAL AFRICAN REPUBLIC) 967
916.76 UGANDA 967.6
914.16 Ulster 941.6
914.161 Northeast area 941.61
914.169 REPUBLIC OF IRELAND COUNTIES 941.69
914.165 Southeast area 941.65
914.166 Southern area 941.66
914.62 Western area 941.62
914.7 UNION OF SOVIET SOCIALIST REPUBLICS 947
916.2 UNITED ARAB REPUBLIC 962
914.1 United Kingdom 941
917.3 UNITED STATES OF AMERICA 973
917.5 ATLANTIC SEABOARD STATES 975
917.6 GULF COAST STATES 976
917.7 LAKES STATES 977
917.4 MID ATLANTIC STATES 974
917.8 MID WEST STATES 978

Entries in italics, with the class numbers on the left, denote classes thought to be most suitable for primary and middle schools. Entries referring to places (except for the ancient world) will be found in the index of places (preceding this index), which covers geography, history, description and travel.

G

Luimneach
Colaiste Oideachais Mhuire Gan Smal